D1304853

DUMONT'S LEXICON OF
ROSES
Varieties · Origin · Use · Care

Andrea Rausch

Photographs by
Annette Timmermann

REBO
PUBLISHERS

© 2004 Rebo International b.v., Lisse, The Netherlands

Text: Andrea Rausch
Photographs: Annette Timmermann
Typesetting: AdAm Studio, Prague, The Czech Republic
Cover design: AdAm Studio, Prague, The Czech Republic

Translation: Lenka Bauerová for Agentura Abandon, Prague, The Czech Republic
Proofreading: Emily Sands

ISBN 90 366 1695 6

Contents

Introduction   **8**

Roses A-Z

       Old Roses   28
       Bed Roses   66
       Noble Roses   102
       English Roses   124
       Ground Covers   160
       Climbing Roses   190
       Shrub Roses   222
       Wild Roses   254
       Miniatures   268

Index

Introduction

THE HISTORY OF ROSES

Roses have a longer history than any other cultivated plant. Symbols of love and beauty for almost all cultures, primitive forms of our garden varieties existed approximately 30 million years ago. As early as 3000 B.C., roses were an essential part of the emperor's garden in Peking. Christian knights in the Crusades brought these Chinese Roses (*rosa chinensis*) with them to Europe, marking the beginning of rose breeding. The Greeks and the Romans honored roses as the "queens of flowers" and plenty of roses were brought into the decadent palaces of Roman emperors to adorn their debaucheries. A lapse in popularity followed, but roses were soon rediscovered as a medicinal plant by monks in monasteries. The next boom originated after pillaging Christian knights discovered the beautifully smelling *rosa x damascena* and the apothecary rose *rosa gallica* "*officinalis.*" The selection of cultivated roses was augmented over the years by accidental discoveries of various types of wild roses. Local wild varieties, Chinese and Damask Roses, formed the base for cultivation of many new varieties. Empress Josephine, wife of Napoleon I, was very fond of roses and initiated the cultivation of a great number of new varieties at the beginning of the 19th century. With the endless number of varieties available today, we would like to help you chose the right roses for you.

WHICH ROSE FOR WHICH PURPOSE?

You can find infinite forms and colors of roses. But how to choose the right rose variety from this vast offering? We have divided roses into the following groups according their appearance: Shrub Roses are impressive specimens 7 – 10 ft (2 – 3 m) tall. Modern varieties bloom several times per season with simple or compound flowers according to the particular variety. Varieties with overhanging branches are better planted separately, while those that grow upright do well in groups or in hedges.

Wild Roses are the primitive ancestors of our modern Shrub Roses, but bloom only once a year. Very often they are thorny and suitable for natural hedges.

Old or Antique Roses are characterized by their strong, compound, often fragrant flowers. English Roses by cultivator David Austin as well as Romantic Roses imitate this nostalgic old-fashioned charm, and besides, they have many blooms. These are 3 – 6 ft (1 – 2 m) tall Shrub Roses in most cases, but you can also find climbing specimens among them.

Bed Roses grow as shrubs and are 20 – 40 in (50 – 100 cm) tall on average. They are suitable for smaller as well as larger surfaces and are always planted in groups. Polyantha and Floribunda Roses form multiple flower clusters that bloom throughout the season. Up to 4 ft (1.2 m) tall, the frequently blooming Noble Roses, with their big, somewhat fragrant flowers on long stems, can also be included in the Bed Roses group.

Ground Covers, known more specifically as ground covering roses, are used to fill larger areas of land or hillsides, border beds or patios and spice up flower plots. They appear in either creeping, tall or shrubby 20 – 50 in (50 – 130 cm) varieties and their simple or compound blossoms are found in clusters. They bloom once or several times a season according to the variety.

Climbing roses decorate arcades, trellises, walls or old trees. They bloom once or several times a season and very often reach a height of 10 ft (3 m). English ramblers usually grow quickly and can reach up to 66 ft (20 m).

Miniatures are suitable for small gardens and flower pots. Miniatures are also ideal for balcony gardeners. The so-called Patio Roses originated in the United States and belong to this variety. Since these roses have long roots, make sure you have a sufficiently deep pot for them.

Tree Roses and Cascade Roses do not really belong to different categories. Tree Roses are Noble Roses grafted onto the 16, 24 or 35 in (40, 60 or 90 cm) long stems of wild roses. Cascade Roses have stems of 5 ft (1.4 m). These Climbing Roses or Ground Covers are regarded as Noble

Roses. Information on whether long stems are available within a given rose variety is included in the description of the variety.

Flowering season starts in July and continues until late fall for most garden varieties. Some varieties bloom steadily, while others bloom only periodically. These are called once or frequently blooming varieties. Some Shrub or Climbing Roses, as well as Wild Roses, are once-blooming in June or July only.

What to Take into Account When Buying

Since your roses will grow in your garden for years, or even decades, it is important to look for high-quality plants in specialized rose shops, good tree nurseries or suitable garden centers where you can get advice as to height, bloom duration and degree of hardiness. Many cultivators also offer their assortments via mail order. Roses in a supermarket are often stored unprofessionally for long periods and are consequently damaged.

How to buy them

Bare-rooted roses have no root ball. They are often sold in plastic bags and the roots are usually wrapped in moisture-holding moss or some other medium. Protecting the roots is vital because dried-out roots cannot recover. You can buy bare-rooted roses cheaply and there is a wide range of choice available. They can be planted in the fall or spring.

Roses with small root balls are wrapped in netting (which you can compost later) and set in cartons in which they can be planted. The roots are better protected, but the plants are a bit more expensive. They can be planted in fall or spring until the end of May.

Container roses are the most expensive alternative, but you can plant them all year long, except during periods of frost. Their root balls should be well-developed. Accustomed to pot culture, they are also suitable for boxes. Starting in May, you can even buy them already in bloom.

THE BEST LOCATION

LIGHT AND AIR: Most roses prefer airy, sunny places where their leaves can dry quickly and fungal diseases are less likely. Avoid drafty or very windy places as well as locations with no breeze at all, which can cause heatstroke and support the onset of pests and fungal diseases. Some varieties flourish in half-shade, yet they still require sunshine at least several hours a day. They should not be planted in shade or in areas affected by water dripping from trees.

SOIL: Roses are so-called "deep-rooted plants" and their roots should allowed to spread without restraint. Deep-laid, tension-free and ventilated soil is ideal. Excessive water should run off well and there should be no wet spots left. The soil should, however, retain enough moisture not to dry out completely in very short drought periods. Sand-clay sub-soil is crucial at this point. It gives the "hungry" plants enough nutrients. It is necessary to add compost, composted manure or bone meal, together with stone dust or algae lime, to light soil. Heavy soil can be loosened up with such additives and supplemented by coarse sand or gravel.

Roses like neutral to slightly alkaline soil with a pH of 6.3 to 7. You can buy special equipment in specialized shops to measure soil pH. Acidic soil can be neutralized with lime, and soil containing too much lime is neutralized with compost or peat-like products. It is important to remove all weeds, especially rooted weeds, when preparing the soil because it will not be possible to do so later.

If newly planted roses suffer without a visible cause and bloom rarely, perhaps the soil is tired. Therefore, before planting new roses, remember to replace the soil and enrich it with compost, composted manure or bone meal. A "rose-free" fallow time of 6 – 12 months is ideal in such cases.

How to Plant Roses Correctly

Planting time: Bare-rooted roses are best planted from October till the end of November while the soil is still warm. In cold regions, spring, from March to April, is the recommended planting time. For root ball roses, you can extend the spring planting time until the end of May.
Container roses may be planted all year long.
Generally, roses may be planted only on frost-free days in regions where the soil is heavy or the temperature cold. Spring is, therefore, the best planting time. If you receive roses by mail-order service on a frosty day, let them thaw gradually in an unheated, frost-free room before you unwrap them.
Preparation: Before planting, you must water your roses heavily. A water bath for 2 to 4 hours is recommended and during the spring, you can even leave them there overnight.
Prune your roses before planting them. Shoots must be shortened to about 6 – 9 in (15 – 20 cm). Climbing and shrub roses can be longer. Roots too must be trimmed a bit and damaged parts must be removed completely.
The hole for planting must be large with a well-loosened bottom so that you can spread the roots without breaking them and they can grow into the soil. Place a stick in the hole when planting roses with tall stems and put the rose 2 – 3 in (5 – 8 cm) away from the stick. Dig the planting hole 4 – 8 in (10 – 20 cm) away from a wall. Climbing Roses and their roots should be directed away from the wall.

Planting: The cultivation spot must be about 2 in (5 cm) – i.e., about 3 fingers – under the soil surface to be well-protected against frost. Then fill the hole with soil and water well. After the water has soaked in, step on the soil gently several times. Do not forget to water the whole newly planted surface so as not to form a crater near the root collar.

If planting roses in fall, cover the plants with soil to a height of about 6 in (15 cm) so that only the shoot tops can be seen. Protect the roses from wind, sun and frost. When planting, you should add compost, bone meal, a slowly acting organic fertilizer or a reserve fertilizer.

Container roses planted in summer must be watered all the time on hot days because they have not yet formed deep primary roots.

BASIC RULES FOR PLANT SEPARATION DISTANCES

Bed Roses, Noble Roses	12 – 16 in (30 – 40 cm)
Quick-growing Bed and Noble Roses	up to 20 in (50 cm)
Park and Shrub Roses	30 – 50 in (80 – 120 cm)
Miniatures	8 – 12 in (20 – 30 cm)
Climbing Roses	3 – 5 ft (1 – 1.5 m)

CARE

WATERING: When roses have taken root well, the plants get their water from the soil. You should water roses during longer drought periods and young or newly planted roses depend on watering. It is better to water your plants once heavily rather than several times lightly on the surface. The water should slowly soak into the soil. A layer of 1 – 1 ½ in (3 – 4 cm) of compost, lawn cuttings, straw, or bone meal mulch will keep the soil moist. If you loosen the soil regularly, its surface will not harden. Never water roses on their leaves.

Fertilizing: Roses are big eaters. A mixture of organic and mineral fertilizers is ideal to meet their needs. You can buy special rose fertilizers in shops for use in March/April or May/June. Follow the measurements specified in the instructions because roses must not be fertilized excessively. Organic fertilizers slowly deliver nutrients to plants so it is recommended to spread compost, composted manure or bone meal compost around the roses in fall. Long-lasting fertilizers should be used starting in mid-May. In mid-May and August/September, you can use half a handful of magnesium potassium sulfate. Potassium strengthens plant texture and fortifies the roses for the winter.

If needed, add a mineral fertilizer to older, well-rooted roses in early spring. Nutrition is thus delivered to the plant very quickly. Do not use nitrogen fertilizers often for risk of prompting the growth of shoots at the expense of flowers. Weak shoots can be easily attacked by pests. Starting in July, you should use mineral nitrogen fertilizer to help harden the wood in preparation for the winter.

The signs of nitrogen deficiency include weak growth, yellowish leaves and few flowers.

During drought periods, please be careful to water roses heavily after fertilizing. If a fertilizer touches wet leaves, it might burn them.

REPLANTING: If absolutely necessary, dig a new planting hole at least as deep and wide as the old one and water the plant copiously.

Unlike domesticated wild roses, many garden rose varieties are very sensitive to frost. Therefore, it is necessary, especially in cold regions, to prepare them for winter as early as mid-November. Cover the roots of the plant with soil and put branch wood on the rose branches. If absolutely necessary, prune them only slightly during the fall. (Roses should really only be pruned in the spring before the first leaves appear.)

Roses in espaliers or arcades can be covered with fir branches. Cut the tops of high stems by about one third, and cover the crowns and cultivation spots with jute sacks rather than plastic bags. In March, remove the protective covers – ideally on a cloudy day.

PRUNE – WHEN AND HOW?

Many roses need pruning to rejuvenate and stay healthy. Starting in March (in case of late frost, it is better to wait until after a cold spell in mid-May), remove the wood branches and soil covering the lower parts of the plants. The year's principal pruning should take place during this period because damage caused by frost and dead shoots can be removed at the same time.

BED ROSES, NOBLE ROSES AND MINIATURES are pruned 6 – 10 in (15 – 25 cm) each year (3 – 4 or 6 – 8 eyes). Weakly growing roses should be cut more radically, quickly growing Bed and Noble Roses less so. Old and weak shoots need to be removed; frozen ones trimmed down to healthy wood.

SHRUB ROSES need only be lightly pruned to get rid of old or weak shoots. Old and English Roses also do not require heavy pruning. A deep rejuvenating prune is recommended only with massive plants.

CLIMBING ROSES need only minimal pruning after they have bloomed. Besides old and dead shoots, also remove horizontally growing branches. Collateral branches of strong, new runners are cut to 2 – 5 eyes.

YOU CAN PROPERLY REJUVENATE CLIMBING ROSES after 4 – 5 years by pruning them back to the ground after they have bloomed.

WILD ROSES AND GROUND COVERS are not pruned.

TREE ROSES are treated in a similar way as Bed and Noble Roses.

You should prune only overly dense crowns or shorten long shoots on Cascade Roses.

You should leave potted roses with as much leaf mass as possible and remove only wilted flowers and leaves.

SEVERAL BASIC RULES:

- Weak shoots should be pruned back more, strong shoots less.
- Suckers are always removed at the root collar.
- Except for Wild Roses, always remove wilted flowers during summer. Then new flowers will grow instead of hips.
- Always use the same rose shears with sharp blades and never crush the rose shoot.
- Always cut an inch and cross-wise above the eye (bud) from which a new shoot grows.

DISEASES AND PESTS

POWDERY MILDEW: Appears as a white substance on leaf surfaces. Leaves and shoots turn brown and die. As with other fungal diseases, a Field horsetial decoction is recommended. Remove diseased parts and destroy them.

ROSE RUST: First, small, reddish-yellow spots appear on the upper leaf surfaces and spore centers appear on the lower leaf sides. Then the leaves turn brown and die.

BLACK SPOT: Dark and frayed leaf spots are typical before the leaves turn yellow and drop.

APHIDS: They prefer to suck on young shoots and leaves. Shoots and leaves crimp; black spot fungus follows because of sap running. Watering with a cold water stream very often helps.

SPIDER MITES AND CICADAS: You can recognize their sucking spots as small white stains; red spiders leave fine spider-webs. A stinging nettle decoction very often helps.

ROSE-LEAF-ROLL WASP: Its nymphs graze on the lower surfaces of the leaves. The leaves subsequently roll up and die. Pick off the nymphs and squash them.

Fungal diseases are caused by wind-free locations or heavy showers resulting in wet leaves. Excessively fertilized plants are susceptible to disease because of their weak texture. The best prevention is an optimal location and balanced fertilization. Even if helpful insects such as ladybugs, hoverflies or green lacewings are plentiful, there are often also natural enemies in the garden. Simple home-made substances usually help when a plant is minimally attacked. If you cannot get by without using a "chemical club," ask in a specialized shop about a suitable substance not harmful to health-promoting insects. This also holds true for animal pests.

Stinging nettle decoction: Mix fresh or dried plants with 2 ½ gallons (10 liters), or proportionally less, water and 7 oz (200 g) dried stinging nettle, steep for one day and then cook half an hour. Let the mixture cool in a covered pot, filter and dilute 1:5 with water before use. The decoction must stand about 14 days (until it no longer bubbles) and should be stirred each day.

Roses for Balconies and Patios

There is room on the smallest balcony for miniatures and smaller Bed Roses. Tree Roses really catch your eye and you can plant summer annuals or perennials under them. A climber is not beautiful, but it can protect you from the gaze of curious neighbors and passerby. You need a structure for it to climb on, however. Roses like sunshine and mildly circulating air on a balcony or patio as well. The pot should be at least 16 in (40 cm) deep and wide because of the long primary root – a purpose for which special rose pots are ideal. Miniatures grow well in balcony pots, which should be 10 in (25 cm) wide and deep. Pots must have drainage openings and it is best to also put a layer of clay on the bottom. When planting in the pot, make sure that the cultivation spot is about ½ – 2 in (2 – 5 cm) in the soil and don't be afraid to cover the root collar a bit more with soil. A mellow soil, rich in humus and sufficiently fer-

tilized is perfect for potted flowers, saving you fertilization during the first year. It is generally necessary to change pots after 2 – 3 years.

In winter, roses need a bit of protection. First, move the plants towards a wall. Cover soil surface with leaves, branch wood and similar material. To protect roots, wrap the pot with nap fabric. Roses must be watered in frost-free periods.

HARMONIZING COMPANIONS

ROSES AND PERENNIALS...

Roses and Perennials complement each other and form a

harmonious picture. Bed Roses, Shrub Roses and Ground Covers are especially suitable for this "marriage." You must follow several basic rules, however:

• The partners must both prefer sunny, airy places.

• The distance of the perennials from the roses should be about 20 in (50 cm) so that the perennials have sufficient free soil.

• Perennials and roses should be always planted separately, not mixed. This enables better and more effective fertilization. Smaller perennials and roses look best planted in groups.

• Candle-like flowers of perennials contrast well with roses.

• You can enjoy your flowers longer if you intentionally plant early and late blooming perennials together.

Blue to violet flowers match nearly all roses: heath aster, monkshood, bluebell, catnip, globe-thistle, gentle lavender, blue and violet phlox, larkspur and salvia.

Yellow flowers go with red and violet: lady's mantle, goldenrod, euglena, coneflower and foxtail lily.

Red cheers up the community: blood-red cranesbill, red autumn aster, horsemint, knotweed and atropurpureum. Pink to blue and violet: musk mallow, phlox with pink blossoms, perennial mallow and thyme.

Flowers or leaves: white and silver are an ideal combination: southernwood, lavender cotton, white autumn asters or feather pinks, pearls everlasting and freely hanging baby's breath.

Grass adds structure: giant fescule, eulalia, Japanese forest grass, tufted hair grass and vernal sedge.

Roses and Woody Plants
form the right frame for a beautiful rose garden.

- It holds true here too that all plants must have the same location requirements. Do not plant roses too close to each other – let them have enough air. Leave at least 3 – 6 ft (1 – 2 m) of space between roses and woody plants.
- Areas under big trees are taboo because dripping rainwater causes fungal diseases.
- During droughts, roses and woody plants share water reserves. Water them more.
- Evergreen woody plants decorate the garden all year long. Varieties with colorful foliage are very impressive, but they can very easily have a disruptive influence.
- It is very easy to combine Climbing Roses with other climbers blooming in summer – based on contrast and tone, as explained in our small color guide. Try to do so when the rose is several years old. Choose hardy kinds like "New Dawn," "Rosarium Uetersen," or "Santana" for this purpose.

CONSTANTS – evergreen broadleaves and needle-leaved trees: berberis, boxwood, ilex, laurel, mahonia, English yew, white cedar, Japanese white pine, Hinoki false cypress, false cypress, cedar and dwarf-pine.
CHANGING BLOOMING SHRUBS: forsythia, garden syringa, kerria, buddleja, bridewort, rose of Sharon, weigela, gragrant viburnum, ornamental apple and cherry trees.
BLUE ONES: caryopheris, blue spire and blue mountain lilac.

Partners of Climbing Roses: It is necessary to mention fly honeysuckle and clematis. With the latter varieties and the types blooming in summer, those not sensitive to fading are the best choices, for example "President," "Jackmanii," "Etoile Violette," "Prince Charles," or clematis viticella.

Basic Rules for Matching Colors

Roses are available in almost all color shades: starting with white and yellow and continuing to rose, red, violet, and even black-red and green. It is tempting to enjoy all the colors, of course, but because too many colors may have an unnerving effect, you should focus on only a few colors. But which of them can be harmoniously combined? You can combine yellow, red and blue as well as contrasting colors – red and green, blue and orange, yellow and violet. Combining warm yellow, orange or red tones is easy. The same holds true for cold colors such as blue and red which have a blue tinge to them, e.g., purple. Pink matches blue and light tones, violet matches white and silver tones. You succeed most easily with tone-on-tone arrangements; bright colors such as red or yellow should be used sparingly or they can be overpowering. Plants with white flowers and gray or silver leaves

blend nicely with warm and cold colors. For example: white roses especially match reds or blues. It is best to match striped roses such as Rosa Gallica "Versicolor" with roses tinted the same basic color of the stripes. Some varieties change blossom color in the course of blooming, offering us a spectacular color spectrum on their own. The "Pure Caprice" variety, for example, initially blooms straw-yellow, later deep pink and while fading, it is apple green.

The following instructions should help you to use this rose lexicon:

Roses have been divided into groups according to their appearance and usage. Within these groups, they are divided alphabetically according to variety name and wild varieties are divided according to their genus name. Family names are not stated because all roses belong to family *Rosaceae.*

The varieties are sometimes known under synonyms, referred to as 'syn.'

You may find a certain variety listed differently in a rose catalogue. The discrepancy is inevitable because several groups overlap when the roses' appearance and usage are taken into account. Thus, to make each description more specific as well as accurate, the usage is stated with each variety in addition to its preference for sun or shade.

Symbols in boxes indicate the particular characteristics of each variety or genus. The symbols are explained as follows:

Location
☼ sunny
☀ half-shade
☀ shade

Qualities:
❀ blooming once
❀❀ blooming several times
⌇ fragrance
❦ hips

Usage:
🪴 pot plant
⥯ tree rose
✂ vase, decoration
✗ rose recipes

Long-lasting roses have been designated as good cut flowers.
Varieties with strong fragrances are especially suitable for rose recipes.

A BIT OF THE HISTORY OF OLD ROSES

The charm of old-fashioned gardens comes from romantic Old Roses with their dense, full flower clusters, tender colors and strong fragrance. Pure Old Rose varieties arose before 1867, i.e., the official origin of the first Tea Hybrids. However, we also include varieties which originated in the beginning of the 20th century as long as they possess the important characteristic qualities of Old Roses. Most Old Roses grow as bushy shrubs with elegantly hanging branches. Strong flowers make this arch-shaped, flowing form even stronger, but rainwater can discomfit the flowers. Because of their overhanging growth, these roses need lots of room.

The first full exemples of *Rosa Gallica* were brought to Europe by Benedictine monks. The first Damask Roses followed, thanks to the Crusades and others, like *rosa x alba,* came by sea later. The cultivation of roses also spread thanks to the French Empress Josephine. Her rose garden in Malmaison, as well as the rose paintings by her court painter Redouté, influenced the popularity of rose cultivation all over Europe. New rose classes such as Bourbon Roses or several-times-blooming Remontant Roses emerged.

"Baron Girod de l'Ain" Rose
Remontant Rose

ORIGIN: *Rosa x damascena var. semperflorens (syn. R. x bifera)*
Offspring of the crimson colored rose "Eugène Fürst," discovered in France by Reverchon in 1897.

APPEARANCE: Wide, bushy shrub, dense branches, reasonably vigorous, 4 ft (1.2 m) tall and 3 ft (90 cm) wide.

FLOWERS: Dense, full flowers shine bright crimson. Each opens like an oyster, emerging with wavy, white-rimmed petals in graceful disarray. It has an intense fragrance.

SPECIAL QUALITIES: One of the early, multi-blooming varieties strongly influenced by Bourbon Roses. It was extremely popular thanks to its red flowers in the days of its discovery and has lost nothing of its charm today.

USAGE: A decorative, bushy shrub for every garden, certain to bloom several times if the location is optimal. Soil rich in nutrients is essential.

PIONEER VARIETY OF REMONTANT ROSES

Almost all important rose groups were involved in the development of Remontant Roses. The parent was a Bourbon Rose. Hybrid Perpetuals, as they are called in England, have progressed from the once-blooming older variety to the nearly everblooming modern varieties. The appearance has changed as well. While many Remontant Roses grow to be luxurious shrubs with hanging braches, others more closely resemble the compact Tea Hybrids. However, they have, through all mutations, preserved their big, dense, full-flower clusters and their charming fragrance.

"Blanche Moreau" Rose
Moss Rose

ORIGIN: *Rosa centifolia muscosa*, hybrid of Moss Rose "Comtesse de Murinais" with Damask Rose" Quatre Saison Blanc Mousseux."
Cultivator Moreau-Robert, France 1880.

APPEARANCE: Tall, upright, 6 ft (1.8 m) tall and 3 ft (90 cm) wide.

FLOWERS: Dense, full flowers in bright pure white with a strong, pleasant fragrance. They open into flat, cup-like shapes and are divided into four symmetrical parts in full bloom. They bloom only once a summer and a second bloom is rare. Purplish, almost black, ruffled moss catches the eye.

SPECIAL QUALITIES: The white flowers are incomparably beautiful, but the plant is liable to powdery mildew and its flowers are very sensitive to rain.

USAGE: As a Shrub Rose, individually or in groups, it can grow in soil lacking nutrients. This variety can be hung on a climbing structure thanks to its height. Also, it is suitable as a potted rose.

ROMANTIC MOSS ROSES

Moss Roses originated at the end of 17th century as accidental offspring of Pale Roses and were cultivated later. Many varieties arose between 1850 and 1870, strongly influenced by Chinese Roses. The unique grace of Moss Roses is reminiscent of the old-fashioned charm of Old Roses. Their leaves resemble those of Pale Roses and Moss Roses, but the pedicles, ovaries and sepals are covered with a thick, moss-like substance comprised of stiff bristles or fine strands according to the variety. If you touch it, it smells balm-like. Moss Roses grow more upright and stiffly than Pale Roses, bloom abundantly and have an intense fragrance. They are very hardy and resistant to cold.

"Charles de Mills" Rose
Gallica Rose

Location:

Qualities:

Usage:
✗

ORIGIN: *Rosa gallica*, unknown origin

APPEARANCE: Bushy shrub, hanging branches, quickly growing, 4 ft (1.2 m) tall and wide

FLOWERS: Big, dense, full flowers show an unusual color change from dark red to purple. They open into flat, cup-like shapes and sometimes have a dark green eye in the middle. The outer petals form a closed rim. Flowers are situated in clusters and last several weeks. Set against the green leaves, the red seems even more intense.

SPECIAL QUALITIES: This Gallica Rose is distinctive partly due to its excellent fragrance. Flower clusters usually appear only once a summer.

USAGE: A decorative Shrub Rose to brighten your garden. It is also a good choice for hedges. It also tolerates soil lacking nutrients, but it rewards a good location with luxurious growth.

INFLUENTIAL GALLICA ROSES

Hardly any other group has had such an influence on the development of modern rose varieties as Gallica Roses, the oldest garden roses. The pre-form – Mundi – is at home in central Europe. These varieties usually bloom abundantly only once a year. The beautiful, fragrant flowers tend towards strong color shades and they are some-times striped, spotted or otherwise variegated. Shrubs are very hardy, frost-resistant and grow well in soil lacking nutrients. They grow compactly with elegantly hanging branches and since they rarely grow taller than 4 ft (1.2 m), they are ideal for small gardens. True-rooted varieties create many root suckers. If you do not want this, choose a cultivated variety.

"*Comte de Chambord*" Portland Rose

Location:

Qualities:

Usage:

ORIGIN: *Rosa x damascena*, cultivation Moreau-Robert, France 1863.

APPEARANCE: Small, compact, 3 ft (90 cm) high and 2 ft (60 cm) wide

FLOWERS: Big, full flowers with an intense fragrance. They are divided into four parts and open into flat, cup-like shapes. Gray-green leaves further enhance the colors of the flowers.

SPECIAL QUALITIES: A shrub blooming many times, almost without stopping, for a small garden.

USAGE: A small rose that grows excellently in groups, i.e., in beds, on the borders of flower beds or in low hedges. It also grows quite well in sandy soil lacking nutrients. It can be placed in a pot on a patio or a balcony and you can get very nice cut flowers from it.

SIMILAR VARIETY: "Jacques Cartier" wins you over with its deep pink flowers and strong fragrance.

COMPACT PORTLAND ROSES

Portland Roses originated in Italy at the end of 18th century. Because they bloom abundantly until fall, simultaneously spreading a pleasant, sweet fragrance, they quickly gained popularity. They are named after the Duchess of Portland, who brought these roses to England. First, classified as Damask Roses, they had a dominant influence on the cultivation of this variety. Like many other rose groups developed over time, (e.g., Gallica Roses,) many botanists regard Portland Roses as an individual group. They are not very big and are thus suitable for small gardens and flower pots.

"Fantin-Latour" Rose
Pale Rose

Location:

Qualities:

Usage:

ORIGIN: *Rosa x centifolia.* Unknown origin.

APPEARANCE: Bushy shrub, regularly branched, up to 5 ft (1.5 m) tall, about 4 ft (1.2 m) wide. Shoots have almost no thorns.

FLOWERS: Fine, pink flowers with dark centers. Dense, full petals crimp and roll back decoratively, contrasting with smooth, deep green leaves. This pleasant-smelling variety is once-blooming.

SPECIAL QUALITIES: Traditional, pale pink flowers have an intense fragrance resembling that of Alba Roses. You can recognize the influence of Chinese Roses in its leaves and appearance.

USAGE: This nice shrub is an eye-catcher in itself and is suitable for hedges and border beds with woody plants. It is also tolerant of sandy soil lacking nutrients.

SIMILAR VARIETIES: "Reine de Centfeuilles" charms you with its big, pure pink flower clusters and tender fragrance.

MYSTERIOUS PALE ROSES

The luxurious fragrance and beautiful flowers of Pale Roses – also known as Cabbage Roses or Centifolia – are unique. Pale Roses have been regarded as a separate genus before, but gene analysis showed that many varieties have participated in their development: *Rosa gallica*, *rosa damascena*, and *rosa moschata* are relatives, among others. We should thank the Dutch for the plentiful varieties because they cultivated Pale Roses as early as in the 16th century. As for their appearance, Pale Roses seem to be haphazard, but you can shape them well with supporting sticks. They are cold-resistant, but susceptible to powdery mildew. Therefore, a suitable location is important.

"Great Maiden's Blush" Rose
Alba Rose

Location:
☼ – ☀

Qualities:
❀ ☙

Usage:
✗

ORIGIN: *Rosa x alba*. Known since the 15th century, originated probably in *rosa canina*.

APPEARANCE: Bushy shrub, quickly growing, hanging branches, 6 ft (1.8 m) tall and 5 ft (1.5) wide.

FLOWERS: Rose-shaped, white flowers with fine pink touches and a fine fragrance appear in summer. They create a perfect harmony with blue-green leaves. There is no second bloom.

SPECIAL QUALITIES: This variety is called also "Cuisse de Nymphe," "Incarnata," "La Virginale," or "La Séduisante."

USAGE: This shrub is nice individually as well as in groups. It is suitable for hedges and also tolerates half-shade in forest borders. This robust rose also grows in poor soil.

SIMILAR VARIETIES: "Small Maiden Blush" is smaller, at 4 ft (1.2 m), but in other respects, it is identical to its bigger sister.

Vital Alba Roses

Alba Roses, with their beautifully fragrant flowers in tender white and pink tones, are among the most beautiful roses ever. The main blooming period is between June and July. The gray-green leaves are as discrete as the fragile colors of the blooms and, with minimal care, these shrubs can fit in with perennial flowers and decorative woody plants. They mostly grow bushy, with elegantly hanging branches. Some varieties form very long shoots and can climb like Climbing Roses. All of them are characterized by good health and resistance to cold. They also grow in half-shade quite well and need almost no pruning.

"Ispahan" Roses
Damask Roses

Location:

Qualities:

Usage:

ORIGIN: *Rosa x damascena*. The variety, known also as "Pompon des Princes," originated in the Middle East. They were bred before 1832.

APPEARANCE: Bushy shrub, 4 – 5 ft (1.2 – 1.5 m) tall and up to 3 ft (1 m) wide. Shoots have only a few thorns.

FLOWERS: Full, strongly fragrant flowers are fresh, light pink colored. When open, the petals roll loosely back. Flowers appear early in summer and keep their color and full form until they wilt. The blooming period is very long, but there is no second bloom.

SPECIAL QUALITIES: Sporty Damask Roses have an early, very long blooming period.

USAGE: This robust shrub also grows in less fertile soil. It can be planted individually or in groups, i.e., in hedges. As it does not grow very big, you can also use it as a potted plant. Bouquets last a very long time in a vase.

ELEGANT DAMASK ROSES

These beautiful roses were beloved by the ancient Persians and were cultivated on a Greek island as early as 1000 B.C. They arrived in Europe from the Near East during the Crusades. Their tender flowers are always full; the color spectrum ranges from bright white to strong purple. They bloom in big clusters and spread a heavy fragrance. Their gray-green, fuzzy leaves are also very decorative. There are two forms, Damask Roses, which bloom in summer, and fall Damask Roses, which have two blooming periods in summer and fall. The ancestor of both forms is *rosa gallica.*

"Louise Odier" Rose

Location:

Qualities:

Usage:

ORIGIN: *Rosa x borboniana.* Cultivation, Margottin 1851.

APPEARANCE: Bushy shrub, quickly growing, hanging branches, 5 ft (1.5 m) tall and 4 ft (1.2 m) wide.

FLOWERS: Japanese-rose-like, full flowers shine with a warm pink. They grow in big clusters above light green leaves and have a pleasant fragrance. This variety also blooms after the main blooming period.

SPECIAL QUALITIES: This robust, fragrant rose is ideal for beginners because it needs little care.

USAGE: This variety is tolerant of shady locations, looks beautiful individually as well as in groups and is also suitable for hedges. It glamorizes a patio or a balcony as a potted plant. Its lovely flowers last a long time in a vase and are an ideal choice for rose recipes.

SIMILAR VARIETIES: "Boule de Neige" offers fragrant, Japanese-rose-like flowers in pure white. The plant is bit smaller than the "Louise Odier."

Multi-aspect Bourbon Roses

Soon after their discovery, these newcomers surpassed Portland Roses in popularity. Bourbon Roses originated as a random hybrid of the Chinese "Old Blush" Rose and the Damask Rose "Quatre Saisons" on Réunion Island. Called "Ile de Bourbon" at that time, they lend their name to the rose that is also called "Rose Edouard" and "Edward Rose." In the end, they also came to France, where their cultivation continued. The result is a wide assortment of continuously blooming Shrub and Climbing Roses with a flower form very similar to that of their parents: one part is similar to Chinese Roses, the other to Damask Roses.

"Maxima" Rose
Alba Rose

ORIGIN: *Rosa x alba.* Probably a hybrid of Wild Roses *rosa canina x rosa gallica* known as early as the 15th century.

APPEARANCE: Bushy shrub, thick, 6 ft (1.8 m) tall, 4 ft (1.2 m) wide

FLOWERS: Strong, full, fragrant flowers are usually pure white, sometimes with a tender pink touch. 6 – 8 individual blooms create a cluster standing upright above gray-green leaves. Their blooming period starts in June and lasts many weeks. This rose blooms only once.

FRUIT: Decorative, oval hips are to be seen in fall.

SPECIAL QUALITIES: One of the oldest white roses with many names, it is known as "Jacobite Rose," "White Rose of York," "Great Double White," or "Cheshire Rose." As "Bonnie Prince Charlie's Rose," it decorates the coat of arms of the house of Stuarts. It received its name "Maxima" in honor of the Bavarian King Maximillian II.

USAGE: This impressive shrub needs enough space to develop. It is very pretty near a wall or at the back of a flower bed and it looks nice when perennials are planted in front of it. It is also suitable for hedges and forest borders. It is robust and resistant to cold and also grows quite well in sandy, nutrient-deficient soil.

RETROSPECT

"Maxima" was a staple in country gardens in the past. As a typical "farmers' garden rose," it gave them a traditional charm. Wreaths adorning young girls during feasts were very often made from its white flowers.

"Mme Hardy" Rose
Damask Roses

Location:
☼ – ☀

Qualities:
🏵 👃

Usage:
✗

ORIGIN: *Rasa x damascena*. Cultivation, Hardy 1832.

APPEARANCE: Bushy shrub, upright, regularly branched, quickly growing, 5 ft (1.5 m) tall and wide.

FLOWERS: When they open, pure white, dense, full flowers show a green eye in the middle. They are found in abundance and have a lemony fragrance. The blooms contrast sharply with the bright green leaves. This variety blooms once a summer and there is no second bloom.

SPECIAL QUALITIES: This nice, white rose lends a certain elegance to every garden.

USAGE: Planted individually or in groups, "Mme Hardy" tolerates half-shade and less fertile soil.

SIMILAR VARIETIES: "Botzaris" charms you with its bright white, full flowers decorated with a green eye. The plant is 4 ft (1.2 m) tall and 3 ft (90 cm) wide.

"Mme Legras de St. Germain" Rose

ORIGIN: *Rosa x alba.* Unknown origin, cultivated since the early 19th century

APPEARANCE: Bushy shrub up to climber, quickly growing, 6 ft (2 m) or taller, 6 ft (1.8 m) wide. Shoots have few thorns.

FLOWERS: Dense, full flowers are creamy white and have an intense fragrance. They grow in big clusters and are resistant to rain. Grayish-green leaves are in perfect harmony with white flowers. Blooms once.

SPECIAL QUALITIES: White flowers cheer up dark places in your garden.

USAGE: It is suitable as a bushy shrub or a climber even for places in half-shade, such as forest borders or sandy soil lacking nutrients. It makes an elegant frame for ponds or other waters. A good cut rose.

SIMILAR VARIETIES: "Mme Plantier" has creamy, white pompon flowers and grows as a bushy shrub or a climber.

Location:

Qualities:

Usage:

"*Muscosa*" *Rose*
Moss Rose

ORIGIN: *Rosa x centifolia* "Muscosa," syn. *rosa centifolia muscosa.* Cultivated in Holland since 1796.

APPEARANCE: Bushy shrub, quick growing, hanging branches, 6 ft (1.8 m) tall and 5 ft (1.5 m) wide.

FLOWERS: Dense, pink flowers spread a tender centifolia fragrance. They appear for several weeks in summer, but do not bloom more than once.

SPECIAL QUALITIES: The mossy form of Pale Rose is a classic among Moss Roses. It has been mistaken for a typical farmer rose for centuries. The notion of "moss" refers to stalks covered with glands as well as ovaries and petals which seem to be covered with a mossy substance.

USAGE: Individually or in groups, it is an eye-catcher and is also suitable as a potted plant. The flowers look lovely in vases and are also suitable for rose recipes. A suitable location is especially important for these Shrub Roses because they are highly susceptible to powdery mildew.

"Nuits de Young" Rose
Moss Rose

ORIGIN: *Rosa centifolia muscosa*. Cultivation, Laffay 1845. Known also as "Old Black."

APPEARANCE: Bushy shrub, tall, upright, compact, 4 ft (1.2 m) tall and 3 ft (90 cm) wide.

FLOWERS: Velvety, dark crimson-red-brown, small, full flowers really catch the eye. Golden anthers are in sharp contrast with dark flowers that look especially good above deep green leaves. The rose has a pleasant fragrance, is just a bit mossy and blooms only once.

SPECIAL QUALITIES: The Moss Rose with the darkest flowers is an ideal choice for small gardens because of its compact appearance.

USAGE: Planted in groups, this rose is suitable for flower beds as well as hedges. It also thrives in a pot. The plant rewards careful pruning and fertilizing with luxurious shoots.

Location:
☼

Qualities:
❀ ⌒

Usage:
🪣 ✗

"Officinalis" Rose
Apothecary's Rose

Location:

Qualities:

Usage:

ORIGIN: *Rosa gallica*. This offspring of the wild gallica rose has been cultivated since 1310, according to written records, and is known all over the world.

APPEARANCE: Bushy shrub, upright, with hanging branches, 3 – 5 ft (1 – 1.5 m) tall and about 3 fit (1 m) wide.

FLOWERS: Crimson, semi-double flowers spread a strong fragrance. They appear abundantly in summer and bloom once.

FRUIT: Orange, eye-shaped hips.

SPECIAL QUALITIES: Essential rose oil gained from petals has been used for healing purposes and for cosmetics production for centuries.

USAGE: This shade-tolerant rose can be planted individually or in groups, matches loose natural hedges and also looks good as a potted plant. You can grow it as a Tree Rose.

WORTHY ROSE OIL

Genuine rose oil is expensive because about 30 flowers are necessary for just one drop. Red petals especially are said to have stronger stimulant and anti-inflammatory effects. Essential rose oil is used externally as a substance in creams, massage oils and baths. As this essential oil vaporizes, it clears your mind and relaxes you. However, it may cause allergic reactions in allergy-sensitive people. In any case, make sure you buy genuine rose oil. Synthetic oil is cheaper and has the same fragrance, but lacks the therapeutic effects of genuine rose oil.

"Old Blush China" Rose
Chinese Roses

Location:

Qualities:

Usage:

ORIGIN: *Rosa chinensis*, before *rosa indica*. Brought to Europe by Parson in 1789.

APPEARANCE: Upright, bushy, 4 ft (1.2 m) tall and 3 ft (90 cm) wide, it even grows to 8 ft (2.5 m) tall as a climber. Fine shoots have almost no thorns.

FLOWERS: Velvety, sparkling, full flowers look sporty with their silver-rose color and spread a strong fragrance. They appear in dense clusters until winter.

SPECIAL QUALITIES: Among old Chinese Roses, this long/bloomer is the best choice for gardens. As it blooms regularly, it is sometimes called the "Monthly Rose." This variety is also known as "Old Blush" or "Parson's Pink."

USAGE: As a shrub or a small climber, this easy-care rose matches any garden, even tolerating half-shade or nutrient-deficient soil. As a potted plant, it is suitable for a patio or a balcony.

CHINESE ROSES

This rose group spread in China and India centuries ago and came to Europe at the end of the 18th century. Chinese Roses are characterized by the fact that they reliably bloom multiple times per season, often without stopping. "Old Blush" is a parent of many new varieties and luckily, it has passed on to them the positive quality of blooming several times a season. Then cultivators succeeded in combining its consistent and plentiful blooming with brand new colors, shapes and fragrances. Chinese Roses are multi-faceted and are suitable individually as well as in groups. They can be potted as well.

"Pompon de Bourgogne" Ros
Pale Rose, Burgundy Rose

Location:

Qualities:

Usage:

ORIGIN: *Rosa x centifolia.* Unclear origin, probably discovered in 1830 in Dijon. In any case, there is evidence of breeding as early as 1664. This variety is also known as "Burgundian Rose" or "Parviflora."

APPEARANCE: Upright, small, 2 ft (60 cm) tall and wide. Very fine shoots.

FLOWERS: Pompon-shaped flowers are claret to crimson colored and sometimes have pink striations. Dense, green leaves flatter the color tone. Its fragrance is very pleasant. This variety is once-blooming.

SPECIAL QUALITIES: A rose for lovers of unique flower shapes and colors. Its compact appearance makes it an ideal choice for balcony gardens. The small shrub is ideal for planting in pots, planters and plant containers and is also very nice as a border for flower beds or paths.

ROSE PETAL JELLY

Put 1 cup of petals from your favorite roses in a pot and pour 1 cup of water over them. It is best to cut off petal attachments because they leave a bitter flavor. Heat the mixture about 30 minutes and then remove the petals. Now add 2 cups of jellied sugar and juice from 1 lemon to the rose water, stir until the sugar dissolves and most of the liquid has boiled off. Mix petals again into the thick liquid syrup and pour the jelly into small glasses.

Tip: For culinary purposes, use only fragrant roses because they impart a lovely rose flavor to dishes and drinks.

"Queen of Denmark" Rose
Alba Rose

Location:
☼ – ☼

Qualities:
✿ 👃

Usage:
🪣 ✂ 🍴

ORIGIN: *Rosa x alba.* "Queen of Denmark" was cultivated in 1816 by James Booth and has been sold since 1826.

APPEARANCE: Bushy shrub, 5 ft (1.5 m) tall and 4 ft (1.2 m) wide. Shoots have more thorns than is usual with Alba Roses.

FLOWERS: Deep pink, the quartered rosette blooms are always shapely and have a pleasant fragrance. Grayish-green leaves create a sharp contrast. This variety blooms once.

SPECIAL QUALITIES: If you love the fragrance of roses, this nice Alba Rose is the right choice for you.

USAGE: This decorative solitaire shrub also grows well in hedges. It grows in soil containing fewer nutrients, but blooms more weakly. Because it is half-shade tolerant, it can be planted near woody plants. It is suitable as a potted plant and also for cutting.

"Robert le Diable" Rose
Pale Rose

ORIGIN: *Rosa x centifolia*. This variety was cultivated as early as 1850 in France. Its precise origin is not known.

APPEARANCE: Wide, bushy shrub; loosely branched and compact with partly lying shoots 3 ft (90 cm) tall and wide.

FLOWERS: Full flowers with a sweet fragrance, colored in a most interesting way. Their color spectrum includes crimson, lilac and purple with a gray glimmer as well as eye-catching striations. They are very often markedly quartered. They grow above dense leaves and appear late compared to other Pale Roses. They do not bloom more than once.

SPECIAL QUALITIES: This variety is robust, but a bit susceptible to powdery mildew. The best prevention is a sunny, airy location.

USAGE: This decorative shrub is outstanding in a garden as well as planted in a flower pot. It is even tolerant of poorer soil.

Location:
☼

Qualities:
❀ ↄ

Usage:
🧺 ✕

"Rose de Rescht" Rose
Portland Rose

ORIGIN: *Rosa x damascena*. It originated in Persia and came to Europe around 1950.

APPEARANCE: Bushy shrub, upright, 2 ½ – 3 ft (80–100 cm) tall.

FLOWERS: Big, dense, full flowers really catch the eye. They are bright red with a purple hue and fade while they wilt. Rosettes are so densely full they look like pompon flowers. After a long blooming period, the plant flowers several more times.

SPECIAL QUALITIES: This healthy, sensitive variety is ideal for rose beginners because it survives mistakes in care relatively well.

USAGE: Suitable as an individual shrub for use in flower and border beds. Also nice in groups. It is recommended for hedges. Because the rose does not grow very big, it does well in a pot. Decorative trees are especially pretty. Older specimens should be carefully pruned so that they bloom profusely.

"Rose du Roi" Rose
Portland Rose

ORIGIN: *Rosa x damascena*. Cultivation, Lelieur 1815. Probably a hybrid of "Portland Rose" and *rosa gallica* "*Officinalis*." Also known as "Lee's Crimson Perpetual" or "Rose Lelieur."

APPEARANCE: Loose shrub, 3 ft (90 cm) tall and wide.

FLOWERS: Full, red flowers with crimson striations. They have a very pleasant fragrance. Second bloom in fall.

SPECIAL QUALITIES: This old variety has had a big influence on the development of other Portland Roses. It was named "Rose du Roi" according to the wish of King Louis XVIII.

USAGE: This small shrub is especially nice in groups. It is also recommended for lower, loose hedges and as a potted plant.

SIMILAR VARIETIES: Flowers of "Rose du Roi a Fleurs Pourpres" are red-violet up to purple. They bloom steadily without pause.

Location:
☼

Qualities:
🌸🌸 ↵

Usage:
🏺 ✕

"Souvenir de la Malmaison"

ORIGIN: *Rosa x borboniana.* Origin, Béluze 1843. Hybrid of Bourbon Rose "Mme Desprez" and an unknown Tea Rose. It was named after the famous rose garden of Emperess Joséphine and it is also known under the good descriptive name, "Queen of Beauty and Fragrance."

APPEARANCE: Bushy shrub, wide-growing, 2½ – 3 ft (80 – 100 cm) tall, but considerably taller as a climber.

FLOWERS: dense, full, quartered flowers are always shapely. They glimmer like velvet, are creamy white-colored, fading with a touch of pink in old age. They bloom in summer nearly without pause and spread a sweet fragrance.

SPECIAL QUALITIES: Nice weather is necessary for the flower to attain its full glory. Under this condition, this "Oldtimer" guarantees fragrant, floral beauty with a touch of nostalgia all summer until frost. Flowers do not usually open when it is raining and leaves are then susceptible to powdery mildew. Take this into account when choosing the right location.

USAGE: This compact shrub finds its place everywhere as an individual plant or in groups. We recommend it for flower and border beds and also as a decorative potted plant or a nice cut rose.

SIMILAR VARIETIES: "Souvenir de la Malmaison" (or "Climbing Souvenir de la Malmaison") is a climbing variety of this Shrub Rose, cultivated in 1893 by Mr. Bennett in England. This rose blooms mostly in June, but very intensely. Only in very nice summers does it bloom once more and it requires a sunny location protected against wind. Classic rose arcs and trellises highlight its nostalgic charm even more.

"Tuscany" Rose
Gallica Rose

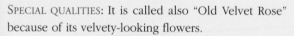

ORIGIN: *Rosa gallica.* "Old Velvet Rose" – as it is also called – was discovered probably as early as 1597 and cultivated in Europe before 1850.

APPEARANCE: Strong, bushy, up to 4 ft (1.2 m) tall and 3 ft (90 cm) wide. If it is planted deeply enough, it grows in width.

FLOWERS: Flat, half-full flowers are a deep, velvety red. Outstanding yellow anthers contrast sharply with the petals. This variety is once-blooming and has a weak fragrance.

SPECIAL QUALITIES: It is called also "Old Velvet Rose" because of its velvety-looking flowers.

USAGE: This shrubby Wild Rose is suitable as an individual plant as well as in groups for large surfaces. It is ideal for planting on hillsides because it helps retain soil.

SIMILAR VARIETIES: "Tuscany Superb" is very similar to this variety. It has bigger, deep crimson-red, fragrant flowers with less outstanding anthers.

"*Viridiflora*" Rose
Chinese Rose

ORIGIN: *Rosa chinensis*, before *rosa indica*. Cultivated since about 1833, unknown origin. Known also as "Green Rose" or "Green Calyx."

APPEARANCE: Bushy, upright, compact, 3 ft (90 cm) tall and wide.

FLOWERS: They are quite unusual for a rose because there are no petals at all. Flowers consist of multi-fringed, green and brown bracts that later turn from crimson to brown. They appear continuously in clusters and have a very pleasant, spicy fragrance.

SPECIAL QUALITIES: This special variety is the right choice for those who like unusual things. Moreover, it only needs basic care and is not disease susceptible.

USAGE: This long-time bloomer is suitable for flower and border beds as well as pots. It can also live in half-shade and in sandy, nutrient-deficient soil. It makes bouqets and arrangements very chic.

Location:
☼ – ☀

Qualities:
✿✿ ୬

Usage:
🗑 ✂ ✕

Turn Flower Beds into Seas of Flowers

Bed Roses are an ideal choice for flower and border beds, large surfaces and hedges. They bring color to your garden from early summer until late fall. They are vivid and have a whole-surface effect if planted in groups. Individually, they are bright highlights. They can be easily combined with perennials, thanks to their natural character. They are sub-divided into two groups, Polyantha and Floribunda Roses. Polyantha Roses originated as hybrids of Modern Roses and after Robert Fortun – the English plants collector – brought Multiflora Roses (*rosa multiflora*) to Europe from Japan in 1865. They have very big flower clusters with relatively small individual flowers which may be simple or full. The plants grow as shrubs with mostly shorter shoots. Floribunda Roses originated as hybrids with Noble Roses in Denmark about fifty years later. The aim was to cultivate robust, frost-resistant varieties that bloom abundantly during even a short summer. Their flowers are very similar to those of Noble Roses, but they very often loose their fragrance. Flower clusters are usually smaller than those of Polyantha Roses, but the plant itself is a bit taller. Passage is continuous with the newer varieties. It is no longer possible to tell exactly to which group – Floribunda or Polyantha Roses – the roses belong. But all of them have common characteristic qualities: they are low-maintence, multiple-blooming, compact with healthy leaves and weather-resistant flowers.

"Amber Queen" Rose

Location:
☼

Qualities:
✿✿✿ ⤷

Usage:
🏺 ⚱ ✂ ✗

ORIGIN: Cultivation, Harkness 1984

APPEARANCE: Bushy shrub, low, 1 – 2 ft (40 – 60 cm) tall and the same width.

FLOWERS: Floribunda Rose with round, deep amber-colored flowers that fade slightly when wilting. They grow in dense clusters and are water-resistant, dense and full, and have a pleasant fragrance. The roses bloom nearly without a break, but there is a clear main bloom.

SPECIAL QUALITIES: This robust rose has very healthy leaves, at first bronze-green, later deep green, leathery and glossy. The yellow flowers contrast beautifully. It was the 1984 Rose of the Year in England.

USAGE: This variety looks really good on large surfaces thanks to its dense flower clusters of unusual color. That is why they are planted mostly in groups of 5 – 6 plants per square meter or yard. It is very pretty by itself, however, and it can also be grown as a decorative tree. It does very well in pots as a shrub or a tree and it is also suitable for cutting.

"Anne Harkness" Rose

ORIGIN: Cultivation, Harkness 1980. This variety is known also as "Harkaramel."

APPEARANCE: Very tall, quickly growing Bed Rose. It is up to 2 ft (60 cm) wide and 4 ft (1.2 m) tall.

FLOWERS: Floribunda Rose with big, dense flower clusters. The individual flowers are apricot-yellow, full and up to 3 in (8 cm) in diameter. The main blooming period is in late summer and lasts until fall.

SPECIAL QUALITIES: It grows very tall although it is a Bed Rose. Its medium-green leaves are very hearty and not particularly susceptible to fungal diseases.

USAGE: Its beautiful flowers make it an outstanding rose for larger areas. Also a good cut flower.

SIMILAR VARIETIES: "Apricot Nectar" roses have small clusters of individual apricot-colored flowers similar to Noble Roses, (3 ft or 1 m) as well as "Southampton" (half-full, fragrant flowers in dense clusters, 3 ft or 1 m). Original "Oranges and Lemons" variety has orange flowers with yellow stripes, 3 ft or 1 m.

Location:
☼

Qualities:
❀❀

Usage:
✄ ✗

"Aprikola" Rose

Location:
☼

Qualities:
✿✿✿ ⌣

Usage:
🏺 ⚘ ✕

ORIGIN: Cultivation, Kordes 2000.

APPEARANCE: Bushy shrub, regular branches, 2 ft or 80 cm tall.

FLOWERS: Bright apricot-yellow fades to light apricot followed by pink. Middle-sized, full flowers are usually situated in umbels, buds are round and orange. Steady blooming with a fruity, herbal fragrance.

SPECIAL QUALITIES: This variety is interesting because its colors extend the assortment of Rigo-Roses® by Kordes. They are robust, but also susceptible to fungal diseases. ADR prize 2001.

USAGE: For flower and border beds, nice together with perennials or low Bed Roses. For looser planting, 3 – 5 plants per square meter or yard, otherwise 6 – 7. Suitable also as trees or potted plants.

SIMILAR VARIETIES: Rigo-Roses® have various colors. "Rotilia" blooms crimson-red, flowers of "Bad Birnbach" and "Fortuna" are bright or tender salmon-pink, "Diamant" blooms white.

"Ballade" Rose

ORIGIN: Cultivation, Tantau 1991

APPEARANCE: Very branchy and upright; 2 – 2 ½ ft (60 – 80 cm) tall.

FLOWERS: Light pink, cup-shaped flowers are round and 3 – 4 in (8 – 10 cm) in diameter. They are half-full, open cup-shaped and when they bloom, the flower center opens. Their color contrasts considerably with the glossy, green leaves. The Floribunda Rose blooms steadily for a long time.

SPECIAL QUALITIES: This variety has a special charm connected with its traditional, old-fashioned flower form. It is very popular not only thanks to its appearance, but also because it is robust and richly blooming at the same time.

USAGE: This is a classical Bed Rose and it also makes bare areas in the sunniest locations quickly green. It is planted in groups with 5 – 6 plants for this purpose. It also looks good in a garden or alone in a flower pot. Trees are also available.

SIMILAR VARIETIES: "Bayerngold" is a pendant in yellow, amply blooming and robust, about 1 ½ ft (50 cm) tall.

Location:
☼

Qualities:
❀❀

Usage:

"Bernstein Rose" Rose

Location:

☀

Qualities:

Usage:

🪴 ⚘ ✂

ORIGIN: Cultivation, Tantau 1987.

APPEARANCE: Bushy and compact, 2 – 2 _ ft (60 – 80 cm.)

FLOWERS: Its rosette-shaped, strong, full flowers in unusual amber-yellow really catch the eye. Also, the deep yellow buds with reddish rims are striking. Big flowers appear abundantly from early summer to fall.

SPECIAL QUALITIES: The "Bernstein Rose" is a modern Romantic Rose characterized by dense, full flower clusters. They are very robust at the same time and resistant to powdery mildew and black spots.

USAGE: This rose is impressive as an individual plant or in groups in any garden. It also grows in sunny places. We recommend a planting density of 5 – 6 plants per square yard or meter. As a tree or a shrub, it also grows well in a flower pot.

SIMILAR VARIETIES: "Blue Parfum" also has dense, full, strongly fragrant flowers of a silvery violet hue.

TIME TO BE ROMANTIC

English Roses by cultivator David Austin are beloved for their big, full, intensely fragrant flowers. At the same time, many other European cultivators – including Schultheis, Tantau, Meilland, and Harkness – offer rose varieties with romantic-looking flowers. Assortments like "Romantic Roses," "Old Master Roses," or "Fragrant Provence Roses" offer you a digest of the best-known cultivators. Accompanying plants should complement the roses in appearance and flower shape. Airy flowers like geranium, lady's mantle, baby's breath and other perennials harmonize with the luxurious blossoms of old-fashioned roses. Violets and feather pinks enhance the romantic character still more.

"Bonica 82" Rose

Location:
☀ – ☀

Qualities:
❁❁ ✿

Usage:
🪴 ⚰ ✂

ORIGIN: Cultivation, Meilland 1982.

APPEARANCE: Bushy, loosely branched, outer shoots hang a bit. Medium-fast growing, about 2 ft (60 cm) tall.

FRUIT: Many round, coral-red hips

FLOWERS: 2 – 3 in (6 – 8 cm) full flowers are light pink, a bit salmon-pink while fading. They bloom mostly in dense clusters of 5 to 10 – sometimes up to 20 blossoms and last a long time. The hips are round and bright pink. This variety is multi-blooming with a dominant main blooming period.

SPECIAL QUALITIES: This variety – winner of the ADR prize in 1982 – is very robust and frost-resistant. It is tolerant of sunny southern exposures or half-shade and also survives cold winter weather without damage. Flowers are highly water-resistant.

USAGE: Very nice alone or in groups for flower and border beds and with perennials and woody plants. It looks beautiful as a ground cover. Plant 7 – 8 plants per square yard/meter or 4 – 5. Suitable for bigger flower pots and cutting. Beloved by honey and bumble bees.

"Bordure nacre" Rose

ORIGIN: Cultivation, Delbard 1973.

APPEARANCE: Bushy, low, 16 in (40 cm) tall.

FLOWERS: Small, dense, full flowers in tender apricot color. They develop in umbels above glossy leaves. This variety blooms profusely.

SPECIAL QUALITIES: This variety, by the French rose cultivator Delbard, was cultivated from the Wild Rose, *rosa canina*. It is very adaptable and is characterized by healthy leaves.

USAGE: As you can guess from its name, this rose is for flower and border beds, but is also suitable for small gardens because of its compact size.

SIMILAR VARIETIES: "Bordure Rose" is a "sister" rose. "Prince Igor" also has French roots (cultivator Meilland). This variety first blooms fiery red and then turns to golden bronze. "Alison Wheatcroft" blooms with full apricot blooms. All varieties grow 17 – 20 in (40 – 50 cm) tall.

Location:
☼

Qualities:
✿✿

Usage:
🏺

"Bright Smile" Rose

Location:

Qualities:

Usage:

ORIGIN: Cultivation, Dickson 1980. Syn. "Dicdance".

APPEARANCE: Low, compact, 18 in (45 cm) tall and wide.

FLOWERS: Half-full, shiny yellow flowers emit a beautiful fragrance. The blooming period is from summer to fall. Flowers reach a diameter of about 3 in (8 cm) and grow in groups. They contrast with light green, glossy leaves.

SPECIAL QUALITIES: Flowers are of a classic Tea Rose character.

USAGE: This compact rose is suitable mainly for small gardens. It is ideal for rose-only flower and border beds, it is not always easy to mix it with perennial plants. You can plant it beautifully in pots and containers.

ROSE TEA

Take 2 tablespoons of fresh or 1 tablespoon of small dried cut petals and cover with 2 cups of water. Tea must steep for 10 minutes and add honey to taste.

"Easy Going" Rose

ORIGIN: Cultivation, Harkness 1999.

APPEARANCE: Wide shrub, 20 – 28 in (50 – 70 cm) tall.

FLOWERS: Floribunda Rose with golden-yellow, loose, full blossoms that keep their warm golden hue as they wilt. Its flowers, in umbels, bloom steadily and present a harmonious picture with the glossy green leaves. The slender buds are very elegant.

SPECIAL QUALITIES: Leaves are not susceptible to fungal diseases, one of many reasons why this variety has received numerous international prizes.

USAGE: This rose is suitable, with its medium-tall height, for small gardens as well as pots, and it can also make large surfaces green.

SIMILAR VARIETIES: "Alison 2000" blooms in shiny golden orange and is shorter than "Easy Going." "Casetta" has apricot-colored, full flowers. It grows 28 – 35 in (70 – 90 cm) tall. "Marie Curie" grows 16 – 24 in (40 – 60 cm) tall and blooms with flowers ranging from copper yellow to golden brown.

Location:
☼

Qualities:
❀❀❀

Usage:
🪣

"Edelweiss" Rose

Location:

☼

Qualities:

❀❀

ORIGIN: Cultivation, Poulsen 1969.

APPEARANCE: Bushy, low, well branched, 16 – 20 in (40 – 50 cm) tall.

FLOWERS: Round, dense, white flowers with yellow centers develop from eye-shaped, yellow buds. They grow in umbels, the individual flowers reaching a diameter of 6 – 8 cm. They contrast sharply with the deep-green, glossy leaves.

SPECIAL QUALITIES: "Edelweiss" received an ADR prize in 1970 as one of the nicest white Bed Roses.

USAGE: This compact rose, planted in groups, is especially impressive. 7 – 8 plants cover 1 square yard or meter very fast. You can combine the white flowers with red blooming roses very nicely.

SIMILAR VARIETIES: Cultivator Noack offers "Schneeflocke," also a low Bed Rose with pure white, full flowers. His long-time bloomer "Brautzauber" grows to 28 – 31 ½ in (70 – 80 cm) and much taller. "Schneekusschen" by Kordes stays very low, at 12 in (30 cm). Its white flowers have a tender pink touch.

"Erna Grootendorst" Rose

ORIGIN: Cultivation, Grootendorst 1938.

APPEARANCE: Bushy, about 20 in (50 cm) tall.

FLOWERS: Blood-red, half-full flowers grow in big clusters above glossy green leaves. They appear continuously until fall and have a light fragrance.

SPECIAL QUALITIES: This variety is very robust and its leaves are not very susceptible to disease.

USAGE: This older variety catches the eye in every big or small garden. According to your desired plant density, we recommend a distance of 12 – 20 in (30 – 50 cm) between plants.

SIMILAR VARIETIES: "Nina Weibull" is a classic. This variety's blooms are also deep red and keep their intense color while fading. Flowers are a classically rounded and cup-shaped when in full bloom. It grows about 20 in (50 cm) tall, is robust, loves to bloom and is very hardy. "Black Ice" is a specialty, with black red, loose, full and slightly fragrant flowers.

Location:
☼

Qualities:
❀❀❀ 〜

"Escapade" Rose

ORIGIN: Cultivation, Harkness 1967.

APPEARANCE: Richly branched, quickly growing, 24 – 31½ in (60 – 80 cm) tall.

FLOWERS: Cup-shaped, loose, full flowers are lilac pink with a white center. Yellow anthers are clearly visible. Flowers are about 3 in (8 cm) wide, have a nice fragrance and grow in dense clusters above glossy green leaves.

SPECIAL QUALITIES: This robust and rain-resistant rose, which blooms abundantly until fall, received an ADR prize in 1973.

FRUIT: Many hips.

USAGE: in groups for flower and border beds as well as low hedges. All combinations with perennials work well. We recommend a distance between individual plants of 16 in (40 cm) and groups of 6 – 7 plants per square yard or meter.

SIMILAR VARIETIES: The blossoms of the "Inge Schubert" are pink to pinkish red with white centers and outstanding yellow anthers. It also quickly makes large surfaces green.

"Flirt" Rose

ORIGIN: Cultivation, Koopmann and Kordes, 2000

APPEARANCE: Broad shrub, heavily branched, up to 24 in (60 cm) tall.

FLOWERS: Medium-sized, loose, full flowers are a remarkable violet-reddish pink hue. The flower center is white, yellow anthers are clearly visible and the individual petals are ribbed. Loose flower clusters grow above dense, light, glossy leaves.

SPECIAL QUALITIES: "Flirt" is an accidental cross of the pure pink blooming variety of "Sommerwind" that you can use as a Bed Rose or a Ground cover.

USAGE: Individually or in groups for flower and border beds. It gives off lots of pollen.

SIMILAR VARIETIES: "Neon," new to the market, has half-full, crimson pink blooms with light centers. It grows 24 in (60 cm) tall and 31 ½ in (80 cm) wide. "Rapsody in Blue" has interesting purple-violet flowers. You can use this variety, with its height of 4 ft (1.2 m), as a Bed Rose or a Shrub Rose.

Location:
☼

Qualities:
✿✿✿

TIPS FOR DECORATION

Fill a bowl with water and floating candles. Sprinkle a few rose petals on the surface.

"Friesia" Rose

Location:
☼

Qualities:

Usage:
🪣 🌱 ✕

ORIGIN: Cultivation, Kordes 1973.

APPEARANCE: Bushy, upright, strongly branched, 24 – 31 ½ in (60 – 80 cm) tall.

FLOWERS: Golden-yellow, full flowers with an intense fragrance. They grow individually or in clusters. While the flowers are classically rounded, the buds are drop-shaped and peaky. The blooming period starts in early summer and lasts until fall.

SPECIAL QUALITIES: This robust, heat-resistant variety is characterized by rain-resistant flowers that clean themselves and keep their color while aging. It is a classic among Bed Roses and received an ADR predicate in 1973.

USAGE: "Friesia" is as impressive individually as in groups. Its yellow flowers shine from a distance and combine well with perennial flowers. 5 – 6 plants are enough for 1 square yard/meter. They also enjoy very sunny places and can survive several days without watering in summer. As a shrub or a tree 35 in (90 cm) tall they are suitable as potted plants.

ROSES IN A BED WITH PERENNIAL FLOWERS

Roses are impressive in a mixed bed with perennials with different blooming periods. Steady-blooming varieties with long blooming periods fall make a good base for such a garden. Give the roses a year's head-start and they can root well before the perennials compete with them. Be sure that perennials and grass do not grow too close to the roses. The distance should be 12 in (30 cm) because roses need open soil and good air circulation. Also, you need some space for the work necessary to care for your roses. For example, stones to step on while walking in the flower bed. The wilted shoots of the perennials should always be pruned.

"Goldmarie 82" Rose

ORIGIN: Cultivation, Kordes 1984.

APPEARANCE: Stiff, upright, quickly growing, averaging 16 – 28 in (40 – 70 cm) tall.

FLOWERS: Loose umbrels of golden yellow, full flowers 3 in (8 cm) in diameter grow in various numbers. Glossy, deep green leaves present a sharp contrast with the blooms. Waved petals make flowers especially sporty. They have a tender fragrance.

SPECIAL QUALITIES: Flowers have a nice display of colors: in early bloom, they are golden yellow with a reddish touch; in full bloom, they are a coppery red and they fade while wilting. They are rain-resistant and last a long time.

USAGE: The outstanding color change of the blossoms is especially impressive if you plant them in groups.

SIMILAR VARIETIES: The golden yellow flowers of "Goldina" are similar to Tea Hybrids. This variety is 16 – 24 in (40 – 60 cm) tall and is suitable for beds and for cutting.

"Gruss an Aachen" Rose

ORIGIN: Cultivation, Geduldig 1909.

APPEARANCE: Bushy, compact, 16 – 24 in (40 – 60 cm) tall.

> **TIP**
> **Dry rose petals give a touch of the romantic to every piece of writing paper. Just glue them on perhaps add a drop of rose oil and then head straight to a mail-box.**

FLOWERS: Strong, full, rosette-shaped flowers are first a tender pink, later creamy white with a yellowish pink center. Inner petals are crooked and the diameter of each tender, fragrant flower is 2 – 3 in (6 – 8 cm).

Location:
☼

Qualities:
❀❀ ↄ

Usage:
🧺 ✂ ✗

SPECIAL QUALITIES: An outstanding Bed Rose with old-fashioned charm. It blooms steadily in summer.

USAGE: A compact variety suitable for the smallest flower and border beds. About 6 – 8 plants are ideal for one square yard or meter for the desired density of plants. It is also ideal for a balcony or a patio because it grows well in pots and spreads its fragrance well. The blossoms are suitable as cut flowers and the petals are good for creative work at home: liqueurs, marmalades and other concoctions.

"Heckenfeuer" Rose

Location:
☼

Qualities:
❀❀ ↄ

ORIGIN: Cultivation, Kordes 1984.

APPEARANCE: Heavily branched, very dense, up to 20 in (50 cm) wide and tall.

FLOWERS: conspicuously blood-red with orange gloss. Cupped flowers are full, petals overlap and the center is open. They grow in umbels above slightly glossy leaves and have a tender fragrance.

SPECIAL QUALITIES: The blooming period lasts until the first frost. Individual flowers are long-lasting.

USAGE: Ideal for for beds and low hedges because of their regular growth. The distance between the individual plants should be 12 – 16 in (30 – 40 cm).

"Heckenzauber" Rose

ORIGIN: Cultivation, McGredy. Syn. "Sexy Rexy."

APPEARANCE: Bushy, quickly growing, up to 28 in (70 cm) tall.

FLOWERS: Full, Japanese-Rose-shaped flowers are pink before they fade while wilting. They grow in many umbels that harmonize nicely with the light green, glossy leaves and have a mild fragrance.

SPECIAL QUALITIES: Abundant flowers are exquisite seen from a distance.

USAGE: A good choice for flower and border beds as well as for low hedges.

Location:

Qualities:

> **TIP**
>
> Roses may often become very dry in close hedges, thus providing ideal conditions for fungal diseases. Therefore, try to choose robust varieties. Besides "Heckenzauber," another tough variety is "Ballerina" – cultivated as early as 1937. It grows with hanging branches and its simple, pink flowers appear repeatedly.

"La Sevillana" Rose

ORIGIN: Cultivation, Meilland 1978.

APPEARANCE: Loosely branched, quickly growing, 28 – 35 in (70 – 90 cm) tall.

FLOWERS: Scarlet-reds and effervescent orange-reds harmonize strikingly with deep green, glossy leaves. Flowers are half-full, 2 – 2 ½ in (6 – 7 cm) in diameter with 3 – 5 blossoms in loose umbels. The hue stays an intense red for a long time, but the flowers suffer under heavy rain.

FRUIT: Plenty of hips.

SPECIAL QUALITIES: This robust, very cold-resistant longtime-bloomer is characterized by a shrubby, wild-rose-like appearance. Additionally, it is heat-resistant and not susceptible to powdery mildew and black spot. It was awarded an ADR premium in 1979.

USAGE: The shrub looks – as an individual or in groups – very good in front of woody plants, in hedges or you may combine it with perennials. White and blue flowers match the strong red rose

TIP

You can form either a formal or quite natural rose hedge. If you do not cut it, birds will enjoy ripe hips. They also build their nests in low hedges. If you like it colorful, you can combine varieties of different colors, but with the same type of appearance.

best. Keep the distance between the individual plants at 16 in (40 cm). It sheds lots of pollen.

ROSE HIP LIQUEUR IN TWO VARIANTS

Recipe 1: Fill 1 quart bottle ¾ full of rose hips and add a bottle of corn-brandy or wine-brandy. Put in a sunny place for 6 weeks and shake every day. Then filter and add 7 table-spoons of sugar. Let the liqueur infuse for 14 more days before drinking it.

Recipe 2: Clean 2 cups of rose hips, crush with seeds inside and put them to a pot together with 1 cup of fragrant rose petals, 1 cup of white sugar and 1 bottle of fruit-brandy. Let it all infuse in a warm place for 4 – 6 weeks and shake every day. Filter and let it infuse for a few more days.

"Leonardo da Vinci" Rose

ORIGIN: Cultivation, Meilland 1993.

APPEARANCE: Bushy, upright, well branched, 24 – 32 in (60 – 80 cm) tall.

FLOWERS: Full, pink, rosette-shaped flowers in the shape of Old Roses. They have only a weak fragrance, but bloom beautifully, often for a long main period in summer.

SPECIAL QUALITIES: Combines old-fashioned flower shape with a compact appearance and non-susceptible leaves. Grows in sunny places as well as in half-shade.

USAGE: This variety is truly multi-faceted and you can plant it individually or in groups. It matches formal beds and gardens well. It is also available as a decorative tree with a height of 24 – 34 in (60 – 90 cm), and it thrives in bigger planters as well. The flowers last a long time in a vase.

SIMILAR VARIETIES: The creamy-yellow blooming variety, "Tchaikovski," belongs in this group of Romantic Roses alongside the full, yellow flowers of the Noble Rose "Michelangelo" and the deep red "Traviata."

Rose "Lili Marleen"

ORIGIN: Cultivation, Kordes 1959.

APPEARANCE: Bushy, branchy, upright, 20 – 28 in (50 – 70 cm) tall.

FLOWERS: Their velvety, blood-red color is impressive. Flowers are cupped, loosely packed and about 3 ½ in (9 cm) in diameter. Up to 15 flowers grow in umbels and contrast nicely with the matte green leaves. The drop-shaped buds are also deep red. They have a weak fragrance.

SPECIAL QUALITIES: This beloved, abundantly blooming variety needs an optimal location and special care.

USAGE: A shrubby, flower and border bed rose also suitable for large surfaces. Plant each 16 in (40 cm) apart. Add a few white roses to bigger groups, for example the "Schneesturm," "Schneekönigin," or the somewhat taller "Schneewittchen" varieties.

SIMILAR VARIETIES: It is recommended that lovers of dark red hues choose, "Mariandel" (dark blood-red, up to 24 in/60 cm tall) or "Lübecker Rotspon" (bright claret red, 25 in/60 cm).

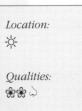

Location:
☼

Qualities:
❀❀ ⸎

"Manou Meilland" Rose

Location:
☼

Qualities:

Usage:
✗

ORIGIN: Cultivation, Meilland 1978.

APPEARANCE: Bushy shrub, amply branched, upright, and grows moderately quickly, 20 – 28 in (50 – 70 cm) tall.

FLOWERS: Strong lilac pink; initially a bit more red in efflorescence. Peaky, drop-shaped buds are red. Intensely fragrant flowers are densely packed with about 50 slightly rolled petals. Their diameter is up to 4 in (10 cm).

SPECIAL QUALITIES: The sporty variety is suitable for warm as well as cold locations.

USAGE: Suitable for flower as well as border beds, outstanding in combination with perennial flowers. Plant 6 – 7 plants per square yard/meter.

SIMILAR VARIETIES: "Anthony Meilland" charms you with bright yellow flower cups; "Matthias Meilland," with its bright red flowers and looks very good from a distance. The shrubby plant is very robust and is also a good choice for cold regions.

BORDERING ROSE BEDS

If you do not want to border rose beds or decorative tree rose beds with the usual box-wood, choose perennials. Perennial plants with grey or white panniform leaves harmonize with all roses. Their soft floral carpet provides an excellent forefront and creates a good passage to other plots in your garden. Lavender cotton (*santolina chamaecyparissus*) or southernwood (*artemisia varieties*) are particularly good selections. The blue-violet flowers of catmint (*nepeta x faassenii*) also match many roses, especially red and pink varieties. These bordering roses bloom in fall even a second time, if you prune them after the first bloom.

"Muttertag" Rose

Location:

Qualities:

Usage:

ORIGIN: Cultivation, Grootendorst 1950.

APPEARANCE: Wide branched, bushy shrub; quick-growing; only 12 – 16 in (30 – 40 cm) tall.

FLOWERS: Bright red in full bloom, but faded when wilting. Flowers are ball-shaped, loosely packed, and, with their diameter of 1 in (3 cm), relatively small. The clusters consist of many individual flowers, ranging from about 20 in the first early summer bloom to up to 10 later.

SPECIAL QUALITIES: "Muttertag" is prevalent everywhere, which explains why this variety is also known abroad as "Mothers Day," "Fête de Mère," or "Morsdag."

USAGE: We recommend this small rose for flower and border beds, graves, pots or planters. In flower beds, plant each about 12 in (30 cm) apart.

SIMILAR VARIETIES: The "masculine" opposite is "Vatertag." This variety is about 10 – 14 in (25 – 35 cm) tall and has loosely packed flowers of salmon-orange.

"NDR 1 Radio Niedersachsen Rose"

ORIGIN: Cultivation, Kordes 1996.

APPEARANCE: Bushy shrub, upright, quickly growing, 32 – 47 in (80 – 120 cm) tall.

FLOWERS: Pink in full bloom, faded when wilting. Cupped individual flowers are half-full and grow in big umbels of up to 15 blossoms. They appear continuously and are weather-resistant and self-cleaning. They are accompanied by a tender Wild Rose fragrance. Deep-green, highly glossy leaves create a fine color contrast.

Location:
☼ – ☀

Qualities:
✿✿ ↝

Usage:
🪴

SPECIAL QUALITIES: This robust rose is not only beautiful, but also has one very special quality: a part of the profit from its sales supports the Rosarium in Sargenhausen.

USAGE: You can plant the rose individually or in groups. Because it grows very large, 3 – 4 plants are enough for one square yard/meter. It tolerates sunny as well as half-shade locations; it is very frost-resistant and easy to care for. It is an impressive spectacle as a potted plant.

"Nostalgie" Rose

Location:

Qualities:

Usage:

ORIGIN: Cultivation, Tantau 1995.

APPEARANCE: Upright, bushy shrub, 32 – 40 (80 – 100 cm) tall.

FLOWERS: a lovely, old-fashioned Noble Rose with full, creamy white and cherry-red flowers with a beautiful fragrance. Flowers contrast with black-green leaves. This variety is multiple-blooming with a long main blooming period.

SPECIAL QUALITIES: "Nostalgie" belongs, with its ball-shaped flowers, to the Romantic Roses. This variety looks in size and shape almost like a Shrub Rose, but it is especially recommended for flower beds.

USAGE: You can plant it either individually or in groups. Decorative trees are available with a stem-height of 35 in (90 cm). They are suitable as a shrub or a potted tree; in a vase, flowers are long-lasting.

SIMILAR VARIETIES: Red and white striped flowers of "Philatelie" look like they were hand-painted (24 – 32 in/60-80 cm tall) and they appear individually or in umbels.

"Queen Mother" Rose

ORIGIN: Cultivation, Kordes 1998.

APPEARANCE: Bushy, compact, about 28 in (70 cm) tall.

FLOWERS: A multi-blooming Floribunda Rose with light pink, half-full flowers and a sweet fragrance. Flowers are situated above deep-green, glossy leaves. Their yellow anthers are very clearly visible in the center of the flowers.

SPECIAL QUALITIES: This popular variety has received, besides an ADR premium in 1996, many other international prizes.

USAGE: A compact variety for flower and border beds. You can enjoy the sporty flower on a potted plant on a balcony as well.

Location:
☼

Qualities:
🌼🌼 ⌇

Usage:
🗑 ✗

TIP

Hardly any rose spreads as many fragrance nuances as this rose. The essential oils responsible are to be found on petal gland cells, sometimes also on leaves, buds or stalks. They develop their full aroma most strongly in the morning and only in sunny locations.

"Rosenprofessor Sieber" Rose

Location:
☼ – ☼

Qualities:
✿✿ ♪

Usage:
🪴

ORIGIN: Cultivation, Kordes 1997.

APPEARANCE: Bushy, 24 – 32 in (60 – 80 cm) tall.

FLOWERS: Pure pink, full flowers of the Floribunda type, their color changes to porcelain reddish pink in efflorescence. They spread a tender Wild Roses fragrance and appear without pause till fall. Rain-resistant flower umbels are situated above deep green, glossy leaves.

SPECIAL QUALITIES: The variety was dedicated to the rose expert, Professor Sieber, and in 1996 received an ADR guarantee of a healthy, hearty and happily-blooming rose.

USAGE: This variety is suitable individually or in groups for flower and border beds. 4 – 5 plants per square yard/meter are enough because of their bushy appearance. A good choice for graves and also grows well as a potted plant. It enjoys very sunny as well as half-shady places.

SIMILAR VARIETIES: "Rosali 83" can be recommended as a happily-blooming Bed Rose with full pink flowers.

"Samba" Rose

ORIGIN: Cultivation, Kordes 1964.

APPEARANCE: Bushy, upright, amply branched, 16 – 20 in (40 – 50 cm) tall.

FLOWERS: Offers an interesting play of colors, combining the basic golden yellow color with bright red on the outer surface of the petals. Red stripes appear on round, yellow buds. Medium sized, light, full flowers grow in big umbels.

SPECIAL QUALITIES: A very good color effect thanks to the bright two-color flowers. They are excellent for decorative purposes.

USAGE: A compact variety for flower and border beds where they are best planted in groups of 7 – 8 plants per square yard/meter. The colorful flowers are most impressive in pure green areas. Suitable for pots and planters.

SIMILAR VARIETIES: The full blossoms of "Rumba" are also two-colored: golden-yellow and orange. First ball-shaped, they open like a cup. Moreover, they have a light fragrance. The plant is 20 – 28 in (50 – 70 cm) tall.

Location:
☼

Qualities:
❀❀

Usage:
🗑 ✄

"Sommermorgen" Rose

Location:

☼ – ☼

Qualities:
✿✿

Usage:
🪴🌱

ORIGIN: Cultivation, Kordes 1991.

APPEARANCE: Wide shrub, partly lying, 24 – 32 in (60 – 80 cm) tall and up to 3 ft (1 m) wide.

FLOWERS: Full, cupped individual flowers are pink with yellow centers and grow in dense umbels. The flowers' color contrasts with the glossy, deep-green leaves. Multiple blooms.

SPECIAL QUALITIES: A robust, low-maintenance rose with rain-resistant flowers. Grows in sunny southern exposures as well as in half shade.

USAGE: You can plant this variety individually or in groups of 4 – 5 plants per square yard/meter. As it is very vigorous, it quickly turns large surfaces green. It integrates well in perennial beds. Almost all other color hues complement its pink flowers, especially blues and violets. You can find such flowers combined with lavender, larkspur, monk's hood, etc. Tree Roses are also available.

SIMILAR VARIETIES: "Sommermond" is a counterpart in lemon yellow, but not so widely spreading

"Trier 2000" Rose

ORIGIN: Cultivation, Kordes 1985

APPEARANCE: Bushy, upright, amply branched, up to 32 in (80 cm) tall.

FLOWERS: Pure pink with reddish borders, an outstanding, active play of colors. Individual flowers are flat and cup-shaped and loosely packed with wavy petals. This gives them a noble character. They bloom in clusters and have a tender fragrance. The drop-shaped buds are red.

SPECIAL QUALITIES: Bushy, robust and weather-resistant Bed Roses with a long blooming time.

USAGE: The strong rose is suitable especially for greening large surfaces. You can mix it with perennials or small woody plants.

SIMILAR VARIETIES: The "Uwe Seeler" variety is a good team-builder and is also suitable for big areas. It grows up to 3 ft (1 m) tall and is shrubby. Full, orange-red flowers have a tender fragrance. "Play Rose," with pink, half-full flowers, is robust and low-maintenance (ADR predicate in 1989).

Location:
☼

Qualities:
✿✿ ↩

NOBLE ROSES FOR YOUR GARDEN AND VASE

When did you last receive a gift of red roses? Give your-self a present: a garden full of blooming Noble Roses for an entire summer. Noble Roses are available in many col-ors and shapes ranging from bright tones or tender pastel colors; elegant classics or romantic shapes; with or without fragrance. Full flowers bloom individually on long shoots with the offspring of Chinese Roses while classic Tea Hybrids and other varieties form side buds beside the main flowers. Decide whether you prefer a cluster of smaller noble flowers or bigger individual flowers. To achieve the latter, simply break the side buds off. Long stalks are ideal for cut roses, while plants up to 3 ft (1 m) tall look a bit gangly in a garden. They have a clear decorative effect in small groups and they are usually planted in threes to fives. It is natural for them to be as close to garden benches and other resting places as possible.

As is often true in life, "noble hearts" are sensitive. The same applies to Noble Roses. They are more sensitive than robust Bed Roses and need a bit more care. You can care best for them if they are planted in pure rose groups or in pots. They are less suitable for colorful accompaniment by perennials and woody plants.

Noble Roses respond especially well to optimal locations.

"Aachener Dom" Rose

Location:
☼ – ☼

Qualities:
✿✿ ✎

Usage:
🏺 ⚲ ✂ ✗

ORIGIN: Cultivation, Meilland 1982.

APPEARANCE: Bushy, stiffly upright, quick-growing; 24–32 in (60 – 80 cm) tall, sometimes a bit taller.

FLOWERS: Big, pink flowers with a silvery gloss are dense and full. Their diameter is 4 – 5 in (10 – 12 cm). They usually bloom individually above glossy, deep-green leaves and sometimes also form several strong, coppery-pink side buds. The petals show an interesting change of color, becoming lighter and lighter towards the center. This variety has multiple blooms, with one strong main bloom, and spreads an intense fragrance.

SPECIAL QUALITIES: This strong, frost-resistant rose with healthy leaves and rain-resistant flowers is also suitable for harsh climes. It received an ADR predicate for its outstanding qualities in 1982.

USAGE: Individually or in groups for flower and border beds. This rose is also satisfied with half-shade. It grows well as a shrub or as a potted tree. A nice cut rose.

"*Barkarole*" *Rose*

ORIGIN: Cultivation, Tantau 1988.

APPEARANCE: Bushy, upright, quickly growing, 32 – 39 in (80 – 100 cm) tall. Young shoots are deep red at first and later darken.

FLOWERS: Attractive, velvety, deep red flowers develop from dark red buds. They are full and round, reaching a diameter of 4 in (9 cm). They spread a pleasant fragrance. This variety blooms continuously after the main blooming period in summer.

SPECIAL QUALITIES: The unusual flower color combines with a blooming period stretching deep into the fall. Deep green leaves with a reddish touch help make this rose lovely.

USAGE: A noble and robust rose that can be planted individually or in groups. This decorative pot plant is also available as a tree. Elegant flowers bloom from especially long stalks and are very suitable for cutting. The fragrant flowers, with their intense colors, should be included in any rose recipe, creative or culinary.

Location:
☼

Qualities:
❀❀ ꙷ

Usage:
🗑 ↕ ✂ ✕

"Belle Epoque" Rose

Location:

Qualities:

Usage:

ORIGIN: Cultivation, Fryer 1994. Syn. "Fryyaboo"

APPEARANCE: Upright, about 3 ft (1 m) tall.

FLOWERS: Inner petal surfaces are golden-bronze while outer petal surfaces are a darker tone, in thrilling contrast to the deep green leaves that amply cover the plant. The large, longish blooms have a pleasant fragrance.

SPECIAL QUALITIES: We recommend this rose to lovers of interesting color combinations.

USAGE: for flower and border beds, individually or in groups; good cut roses; fine fragrance.

SIMILAR VARIETIES: "Just Joey" is another interesting color variety. The coppery orange flowers are packed with red striations, the petals are wavy. The plants are 35 in (90 cm) tall and grow vigorously. "Tequila Sunrise" has yellow flowers with red rims and grows about 30 in (75 cm) tall. It is an outstanding Bed Rose. The fragrant, yellow flowers of "Banzai 83" (32– 40 in/80 – 100 cm) also have a reddish rim.

"Duftzauber 84" Rose

ORIGIN: Cultivation, Kordes 1984.

APPEARANCE: Stiff, bushy and branched; 28 – 35 in (70 – 90 cm) tall.

FLOWERS: Bright scarlet-red flowers with a strong fragrance develop from deep red buds. They are full and have a medium-sized diameter of 3 ½ in (9 cm). They mostly bloom individually on strong stalks, rarely in clusters on branched shoots.

SPECIAL QUALITIES: This rose combines a noble flower form with a beautiful fragrance. Its bright red lasts until wilting.

USAGE: This variety has a strong color effect when it is planted in either small or large groups. Decorative trees are especially suitable as potted plants. This fragrant plant is ideal for many rose recipes.

SIMILAR VARIETIES: "Duftwolke" is, with its coral-red, full flowers, a good choice for those who love outstanding rose fragrances. Since it is very robust and frost-resistant, it is highly recommended for cold regions.

Location:

☼

Qualities:

❀❀

Usage:

"Erotica" Rose

Location:

Qualities:

Usage:

ORIGIN: Cultivation, Tantau 1968.

APPEARANCE: Upright, compact, 24 – 32 in (60 – 80 cm) tall.

Flowers: Deep red buds ripen to nobly shaped flowers with a velvety red color. Flowers are full and very large, up to 5 in (12 cm) in diameter. Outer petals roll impressively outwards. The rose possesses a pleasant, spicy fragrance.

SPECIAL QUALITIES: These roses with long stalks are striking in flower beds. Plants should be about 16 in (40 cm) apart.

FACE TO FACE WITH A ROSE

Rose Trees really catch your eye in formal parks as well as in ordinary house gardens and flower pots on balconies or patios. They greet every guest warmly when situated near your front door.

"Focus" Rose

ORIGIN: Cultivation, Noack 1997.

APPEARANCE: Bushy, upright, about 28 in (70 cm) tall.

FLOWERS: The salmon-pink roses are dense and full, with diameters of 4 in (10 cm). Deep green, very glossy leaves that last a long time create a contrasting base for the color of the flowers. The plant also blooms abundantly after the main blooming period.

Location:

Qualities:

Usage:

SPECIAL QUALITIES: This Noble Rose has received many international prizes. It is not susceptible to leaf diseases such as black spot or powdery mildew.

HOW TO PREPARE ROSES FOR PRUNING
With roses that form flower clusters, remove the highest bud before it ripens because if it opens first, the others will stop blooming. Remove side shoots from Noble Roses to yield big, individual flowers.

USAGE: Ideal for flower and border beds, either individually or in groups. We recommend 5 plants per square yard/meter. The rose is also available as a tree and enjoys flower pots.

"Gloria Dei" Rose

Location:

Qualities:

Usage:

ORIGIN: Cultivation, Meilland 1945. It is also known as "Mme A. Meilland," "Peace," or "Gioia."

APPEARANCE: Upright, wide and bushy, very strong and quick-growing, 32 – 40 in (80 – 100 cm) tall.

FLOWERS: Elegant, tea-rose-shaped flowers are first yellow with a coppery red rim in efflorescence, later touched with a tender pink. They are very full, 5 – 6 in (12 – 14 cm) in diameter, and bloom mostly on strong stalks. The long, main blooming period lasts until the fall. They have a tender fragrance.

SPECIAL QUALITIES: The best-known rose in the world charms you with the beauty of its flowers as well as its vigorous growth and health.

USAGE: As a garden and cut rose, "Gloria Dei" always catches the eye. Suitable as an individual plant as well as in groups, it also enjoys half-shade and its flowers do not suffer in heavy showers. As a shrub or a tree, it is suitable for a flower pot. As a cut rose, it is characterized by its long vase life.

HOW TO CUT ROSES CORRECTLY

You should cut roses early in the morning when they are still cold and fresh after the night and thus will last longer. Buds should be slightly open and show a bit of color. Do not cut stalks too long. Do not cut too many: 2 from each plant should be enough.

Before you put roses in a vase, cut the stalks cleanly on a slant and remove the leaves. Then put the flowers immediately into a vase so that they can quickly make up the loss of water.

Roses last longer in vases if you add a bit of sugar and 1 teaspoon of apple vinegar.

"Montezuma" Rose

Location:

Qualities:

Usage:

ORIGIN: Cultivation, H.C. Swim 1955.

APPEARANCE: Upright, quickly growing, up to 4 ft (1.3 m) tall and up to 27 in (70 cm) wide.

FLOWERS: Elegant, full flowers are bright salmon-red and spread a tender fragrance. They have a diameter of 3 in (9 cm) and bloom in loose clusters above bright green, leathery leaves. Blooming period lasts from summer to fall.

SPECIAL QUALITIES: Suitable, thanks to its height, for the back row of rose beds, but it should be easily accessible for cutting since it looks lovely in vases.

USAGE: Individually or in groups for flower and border beds; a good cut rose with long stems.

ROSES LAST LONGER IN A VASE THIS WAY

Change water daily and trim roses on a slant each time.
Never drip water on leaves because it produces hideous stains. After each "rose-season," clean vases thoroughly.

"Painted Moon" Rose

ORIGIN: Cultivation, Dickson 1991. Syn. "Dicpaint."

APPEARANCE: Wide shrub; grows overhanging, up to 30 in (75 cm) tall and 24 in (60 cm) wide.

FLOWERS: Full flowers are usually color: yellow with crimson and pink touches. Subtly fragrant individual flowers are about 4 in (9 cm) wide and appear in clusters until fall. They look good above the dense, medium-green leaves.

Location:
☼

Qualities:
❀❀ ﹀

Usage:
✂

SWIMMING ROSES

The individual blooms in a bouquet of roses never wilt simultaneously. Take advantage of the ones which last longer. Shorten the stems and put the flowers in a short pot. Bird-feeders, fountains or ponds are excellent for this purpose.

SPECIAL QUALITIES: A dense shrubby rose for lovers of two-colored flowers.

USAGE: This compact rose is suitable for rose beds, natural or formal as well as in low hedges. Its flowers are wonderful in vases.

"Paul Cézanne" Rose

ORIGIN: Cultivation, Delbard 1997.

APPEARANCE: Upright, 24 in (60 cm) tall.

FLOWERS: Yellow buds open to loosely packed flowers with tender yellow petals with orange and tender pink stripes. Their fragrance resembles oranges and pears.

SPECIAL QUALITIES: The unusual color of the flowers originating in France brings a feeling of summer and the Mediterranean into your garden and flat. The flowers are very suitable for decorative purposes.

USAGE: The variety is, at 24 in (60 cm), not too tall. Therefore, it works well in small gardens, flower or border beds or bigger flower pots on balconies or patios. You can plant them pretty densely in a bed without worries.

SIMILAR VARIETIES: "Camille Pissaro" (red, rose-pink, yellow and white flowers with an apple fragrance), "Claude Monet" (yellow, striped rose-pink flowers with a sweet fruity fragrance), "Henri Matisse" (rose-red and white striped flowers with a fragrance resembling old farmers'roses). All of them grow 32 – 40 in (80 – 100 cm) tall.

"Polarstern" Rose

ORIGIN: Cultivation, Tantau 1982.

APPEARANCE: Upright, loosely structured, quickly growing, 24 – 32 in (60 – 80 cm) tall, sometimes up to 3 ft (1 m).

FLOWERS: Noble, dense, bright white Tea Hybrids have a tender fragrance. Big flowers develop from drop-shaped buds and bloom on long stems. They continue to appear after the main blooming period. They shine especially brightly above deep-green leaves.

SPECIAL QUALITIES: Elegant white flowers combined with a resistant nature. The rose is frost-resistant and is recommended for colder regions.

USAGE: White flowers brighten flower and border beds either as individuals or in groups. You can also combine this rose well with perennials. Keep plants a distance of 16 – 20 in (40 – 50 cm) apart when planting. It is suitable as a potted tree or bush as well. The long stems of this rose are ideal for bunches and its flowers can be used in many recipes.

Location:
☼

Qualities:
✿✿ ⌇

Usage:
🏺 ⚱ ✂ ✗

"Rosemary Harkness" Rose

Location:

Qualities:

Usage:

ORIGIN: Cultivation, Harkness 1985. Syn. "Harrowbond."

APPEARANCE: Upright, bushy, and fast-growing, 24 – 32 in (60 – 80 cm) tall.

FLOWERS: A Tea Hybrid with full, orange to salmon-orange flowers with a strong fragrance. Flowers appear through the summer until fall with deep-green, glossy leaves.

SPECIAL QUALITIES: A robust Noble Rose of an especially nice color – very striking in beds or vases.

USAGE: This variety is suitable as a garden rose for flower and border beds or as a cut rose for decorative purposes. Excellent for rose recipes.

SIMILAR VARIETIES: "Christopher Columbus" blooms with dense, full flowers of a coppery orange color. This variety is very resistant and low-maintenance and also grows in half-shade and in bigger flower pots. Like "Tea Lime," a coppery golden-orange, or "Kupferkönigin," a coppery yellow, it is ideal for cutling.

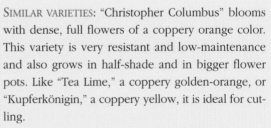

"Savoy Hotel" Rose

ORIGIN: Cultivation, Harkness 1991. Introduced in Great Britain in 1989. Syn. "Harvintage" or "Integrity."

APPEARANCE: Upright, bushy, strongly growing, but compact, up to 32 in (80 cm) tall and 24 in (60 cm) wide.

FLOWERS: A pastel pink, blooming Tea Hybrid whose flowers have a darker pink touch on their lower surface. The full flowers are classic, but slightly ball-shaped and reach a diameter of about 4 in (11 cm). Their blooming period lasts until fall and they possess a tender fragrance.

SPECIAL QUALITIES: An amply blooming variety resistant to rose diseases, praised as one of the best roses by the Royal Horticultural Society.

USAGE: A quick-growing, but compact variety suitable for flower and border beds. An outstanding cut rose. Also available as a tree.

SIMILAR VARIETIES: "Lovely Lady" (35 in/90 cm) has big, full, pink flowers with coral pink shading.

Location:
☼

Qualities:
✿✿ ↝

Usage:
🏺 🌱 ✂

"Schwarze Madonna" Rose

Location:
☼

Qualities:
❀❀ ♪

Usage:
✀

ORIGIN: Cultivation, Kordes 1992.

APPEARANCE: Bushy shrub, upright, 24 – 32 in (60 – 80 cm) tall.

FLOWERS: Full, black-red flowers with velvety gloss have a delicate fragrance and diameters of up to 5 in (12 cm). This variety really catches the eye with its reddish, later deep-green, glossy, leaves. Its peaky, drop-shaped, black-red buds are dramatic.

SPECIAL QUALITIES: A classic beauty in dark red.

USAGE: The rose – planted in groups – fits well in flower and border beds. And it is a natural choice for a vase, especially since it is long-lasting.

BLACK LIKE THE NIGHT

Even though many cultivators wish it, there is no truly black rose. It is perhaps good that nature does not permit us to completely dominate it. As Konrad Adenauer said, "A rose is something so nice that it cannot be spoiled even by the most foolish cultivator."

"Sebastian Kneipp" Rose

ORIGIN: Cultivation, Kordes 1997.

APPEARANCE: Upright, branched, blooms well a second time, 32 – 40 in (80 – 100 cm) tall.

FLOWERS: A Noble Rose with the charm of Old Roses with creamy white and pink flowers with yellowish middles. They are very full and are divided into four parts. Most of them bloom in umbels and have a strong, sweet fragrance. The bright flower color is captivating with the deep-green, glossy leaves.

Location:
☼

Qualities:
❀❀❀ ♪

Usage:
🗑 ✂ ✗

SPECIAL QUALITIES: This Romantic Rose with its intoxicating fragrance was introduced on the 100th anniversary of Father Kneipp's death.

USAGE: This robust rose can be planted as an individual or in groups. It also survives hot southern exposures. You can have it on a balcony or a patio as a potted plant. Its sporty, fragrant flowers are suitable as cut roses, for decorative purposes, and for rose recipes.

SIMILAR VARIETIES: "Sweet Lady" (20 – 28 in/50 – 70 cm tall) has full, creamy caramel-colored, fragrant flowers.

"Silver Jubilee" Rose

ORIGIN: Cultivation, Cocker 1978.

APPEARANCE: Upright, bushily branched, 20 – 28 in (50 – 70 cm) tall. Shoots have many thorns.

FLOWERS: Pink, dense and full Tea Hybrids with a tender fragrance. Big flowers appear early in summer and continuously after that. If you remove side buds of flower clusters, huge individual flowers bloom, reaching diameters of 4 – 5 in (10 – 12 cm). Leaves are glossy green and contrast sharply with the various pink shades of blossoms.

SPECIAL QUALITIES: An especially robust and richly blooming variety characterized by rain-resistant flowers. It even tolerates soil lacking nutrients and half-shady locations. It was named for the 25th anniversary of the coronation of Queen Elisabeth II.

USAGE: Plant this rose in groups in your garden so it can appear at its best. It enriches every bed and is also recommended for loose hedges. A tree variety, available for planting in pots, reaches 24 – 35 in (60 or 90 cm) in height. Flowers last a long time in a vase.

SMALL VARIETIES: "Piroschka" is bright, pure pink, accompanied by a strong fragrance.

A VASE IS NOT ALWAYS REALLY A VASE

In order for roses to last a long time, stems must be deeply immersed in water. Therefore, use the deepest pots, vases, jars or tea or coffee cans available. The container's shape and color should not be so eye-catching as to distract attention from the roses. Glass vases are neutral and do not hide the very often decorative stems with thorns.

"Typhoon" Rose

Location:

Qualities:

Usage:

ORIGIN: Cultivation, Kordes 1972. Syn. "Taifun."

APPEARANCE: Upright, regularly overhanging, up to 30 in (75 cm) tall and 26 in (65 cm) wide.

FLOWERS: A Tea Hybrid with ball-shaped, full flowers showing a color spectrum ranging from salmon-pink to orange-red and contrasting delectably with the deep-green, glossy leaves. Fragrant flowers can be up to 4 in (10 cm) wide and bloom through the summer until fall.

SPECIAL QUALITIES: Its charming color scheme makes this variety very interesting as a garden or cut rose.

USAGE: For rose beds, as a cut flower, for decorative purposes and manual creative work.

ROSE PETAL PRESSING
Strong or unusual colors are especially suitable for rose petal pressing and you do not need many tools. Just put leaves between the pages of a thick book, e.g., a phone directory which you no longer use. Put other books on top to add weight and wait until the petals are dry.

"Valencia" Rose

ORIGIN: Cultivation, Kordes 1989. Syn. "Koreklia."

APPEARANCE: Upright, loosely bushy, but compact shrub; up to 28 in (70 cm) tall and 24 in (60 cm) wide.

FLOWERS: Classic Tea Hybrids with full, fragrant, amber yellow flowers tinged with red. They grow to 4 in (10 cm) across, bloom on long, strong stems and have a very intense fragrance. The brilliance of the blooms is enhanced by the color of the dark green leaves through the summer until fall.

SPECIAL QUALITIES: A Noble Rose of outstanding elegance. Thanks to its pleasant fragrance, it was praised as the most fragrant rose.

USAGE: Plant this attractive rose in groups in natural or formal flower and border beds. It is perfectly suitable for cutting. And it also emits its beautiful fragrance indoors.

SIMILAR VARIETIES: "Sutter's Gold" (up to 3 ft/1 m tall) blooms golden-yellow with a reddish tinge.

Location:
☼

Qualities:
✿✿ ◡

Usage:
✄ ✕

ROMANTIC APPEAL OF ENGLISH ROSES

Old Roses were almost banished from gardens when abundantly blooming Tea Hybrids appeared. But the modern varieties could not completely replace the charm and antique fragrance of older flowers. At the same time, the color spectrum, abundant blossoms and robustness of Tea Hybrids set a new standard. Recently English cultivator David Austin created a work of art by crossing Old Roses with modern Tea Hybrids and Floribunda Roses, combining romantic, old-fashioned flower shapes and fragrances with the qualities of modern, robust garden roses. He also added many new colors that were not available before. His "English Roses" have become staples of rose assortments. The dense, full flowers of English Roses do not bloom just once, but many times a year. Moreover, they have a beautiful fragrance. Most varieties grow as big shrubs; others can be used as bed or climbing roses or to glamorize your balcony or your patio as potted plants. They are not as susceptible as Old Roses to diseases and showers, thanks to their robust leaves. You only need a few plants to inspire a romantic mood!

"Abraham Darby" Rose

Location:

Qualities:

Usage:
🗑 ✂ ✗

ORIGIN: Cultivation, Austin 1985.

APPEARANCE: Quick-growing Shrub Rose with well-shaped, overhanging branches. It grows very quickly and up to 5 – 7 ft (1.5 – 2 m) tall.

FLOWERS: The colors of these extremely full flowers range from pink to orange to apricot. The plants spread a strong, fruity, herbal fragrance. They bloom profusely until the end of the season and the main blooming period occurs in early summer.

SPECIAL QUALITIES: Petals are tinted yellow on their inner surfaces. When they roll up, they show an especially interesting play of yellow and pink tones. With its big flowers, this variety is unusually charming.

USAGE: A rose romantic might be charmed by this rose individually or in groups. Individual plants provide highlights while groups have a stronger color effect. The hanging branches look especially good if planted less densely and in smaller numbers. 1 – 2 plants are enough for one square yard/meter. This rose is also grown as a climber, thanks to its long shoots. At the same time, it is suitable as

a potted plant and for cutting. Be sure to choose an appropriate location for this rose, as it is sometimes a bit susceptible to rose rust. The fragrant flowers are also recommended for rose recipes.

NO PARTY WITHOUT A ROSE BOWL

Heat 2 cups of water with 1 cup of sugar and then add 2 full cups of rose petals. The whole thing must be cooled in a covered pot so that its aroma does not escape. Pour into a bowl, add 7 tablespoons of lemon juice and 2 bottles of red or white champagne, mix and the party drink is ready. Mix well before serving and decorate with several rose petals.

"Belle Story" Rose

Location:

Qualities:

Usage:
🗑 ✄ ✗

ORIGIN: Cultivation, Austin 1984.

APPEARANCE: Upright, bushy, loosely branched, 4 ft (1.2 m) tall and wide.

FLOWERS: The gentle pink of the petals becomes lighter towards the edges. The flowers themselves are very symmetrical and look dainty in spite of their size. When they open, they reveal yellow anthers in the middle. This rose smells like Tea Roses.

SPECIAL QUALITIES: With its big, open flowers, this rose looks almost like a peony. It cannot be mistaken for it though, thanks to its bright leaves and characteristic rose fragrance.

USAGE: This bush is an eye-catcher alone as well as in groups. Three plants form a very nice group. Planted in rows, "Belle Story" forms romantic hedges. It is a nice potted plant and cut flower as well.

SIMILAR VARIETIES: "Barbara Austin," with its lilac-like scent, could be recommended to lovers of tender pinks.

A Little Fragrance Science

No rose has the same fragrance and scents are subjectively perceived. Nevertheless, we can divide fragrances of English Roses into four groups, with some overlap, of course:

The myrtle-like fragrance is strongly spicy. It probably originated from an old climbing rose called "Ayrshire Splendens." "Constance Spry" inherited it.

The fragrance of Old Roses lies heavy and sweet in the air. It is especially strong with "Gertrude Jekyll" and "The Prince."

The charming fragrance of Tea Roses is reminiscent of fresh tea leaves. "Graham Thomas" is a well-known example.

The fruity herbal smell makes you think of freshly picked apples. Try a sniff of "Leander."

"Charles Austin" Rose

Location:
☼

Qualities:
🌸🌸

Usage:
🗑 ✂ ✗

ORIGIN: Cultivation, Austin 1963.

APPEARANCE: Bushy shrub, upright, quickly growing, 3 – 5 ft (1 – 1.5 m) tall, 4 ft (1.2 m) wide.

FLOWERS: Cupped, dense, full flowers come in various apricot tones that fade while wilting. They are tightly packed and built like a quartered rosette. They are accompanied by an intense fragrance. This variety blooms several times within a main blooming period.

SPECIAL QUALITIES: "Charles Austin" is characterized by very big, rosette-shaped, unusually colored flowers and a fruity fragrance.

USAGE: You can plant the shrub individually, but it is much more striking in groups. 1 -2 plants are enough for one square yard/meter, thanks to their size. It is recommended to rejuvenate them occasionally so that they do not warp. This variety is suitable as a potted plant and its flowers last a long time in a vase and are ideal for rose recipes.

SIMILAR VARIETIES: "Yellow Charles Austin" is the yellow counterpart with the same qualities.

ROMANTIC BUNCHES WITH ENGLISH ROSES

With their natural beauty and charming fragrance, Romantic Roses are among the most beautiful flowers for cutting. One individual bouquet is enough to fill the whole room with fragrance. To ensure that the flowers last a long time, cut them early in the morning and immediately put them into water. If the buds are cut half-open, they will open fully in the vase. English Roses look best in natural arrangements. Just let the bunch glide into the vase because the luxurious, heavy flowers tend to shape themselves. Naturally, you can add individual flowers to the bunch or change the arrangement. The tender colors of the flowers almost always harmonize with one another. You can make bouquets of various colors or create sharp contrasts.

"Charles Rennie Mackintosh Rose

Location:
☼

Qualities:
✿✿ ᓇ

Usage:
🗑 🍴 ✂ ✗

ORIGIN: Cultivation, Austin 1988.

APPEARANCE: Upright, bushy, and strong, but compact, growing to 35 in (90 cm) tall and 30 in (75 cm) wide.

FLOWERS: The densely packed flowers have a pleasant lilac-pink shine. Inner, rolled petals are a lovely touch. This variety blooms almost without break until fall and gives off a strong rose fragrance.

SPECIAL QUALITIES: The variety is resistant to wind and weather. The clear lilac color of the flower petals looks charming above the small, dark-green leaves.

USAGE: A healthy, robust rose for mixed flower and border beds, with a compact appearance ideal for small gardens. Thin shoots with many thorns quickly create thick hedges. Thanks to the color of its flowers, this variety harmonizes beautifully, especially with other English Roses. The big flower balls are wonderful for rose arrangements.

MIXED BORDER – ENGLISH ROSES IN MIXED BORDER BEDS

English roses are ideal components of colorful, durable beds when mixed with woody plants, perennials and annuals. The partner plants must complement each other in color as well as in height and shape. Very tall varieties like "Charles Austin" belong in the background. Continuous passages can be achieved, e.g., with overhanging shoots, such as "Abraham Darby." Lower, bushy varieties such as the "Charles Rennie Mackintosh" or "Wife of Bath" are suitable especially for the front of a border bed. Long, tall flowers, such as lavender, salvia or speedwell create thrilling contrasts to the round flower balls of roses.

"Constance Spry" Rose

Location:
☼ – ☀

Qualities:
❀ ⌣ ❀

Usage:
✂ ✗

ORIGIN: Cultivation, Austin 1960.

APPEARANCE: Bushy shrub, overhanging branches, wide reaching and quickly growing, shrub 5 – 6 ½ ft (1.50 – 2 m) tall and about 5 ft (1.5 m) wide and much taller as a climber.

FLOWERS: Pink petals fade towards the rim. The flowers are dense and full and have a diameter of 5 in (12 cm). They bloom along shoots and smell like myrtle. They contrast nicely with their gray-green leaves. Blooms once in June/July.

FRUIT: They form many big, orange hips.

SPECIAL QUALITIES: This variety is the first English Rose of British cultivator David Austen: a cross between the Gallica Rose "Belle Isis" and the Floribunda Rose "Dainty Maid." It is characterized by unusual, ball-shaped flowers similar to peonies. Its blooming period is relatively short, however.

USAGE: Whether individually or in groups, this variety is always a nice sight. It is recommended to provide bushes covering 2 square yards/meters. If you plant groups in

a bed, 1 – 2 roses per square yard/meter should suffice
according to how dense you want the planting to be. It is
a good climber, with long stalks that are best guided on
a fence or a trellis. Moreover, they quickly form dense
hedges with their thorny branches. "Constance Spry"
grows in hot southern exposures as well as in half-shade,
also tolerating nutrient-deficient soil. To grow this variety
well, we recommend occasional pruning to rejuvenate it.
It is a good cut rose and the flowers are excellent for rose
recipes.

SIMILAR VARIETIES: The "Chianti" Shrub Rose has wine-red
pendant blooms. It grows 5 – 6 ft (1.5 – 1.8 m) tall and
about 4 ft (1.2 m) wide.

"English Garden" Rose

Location:

Qualities:

Usage:

ORIGIN: Cultivation, Austin 1986. In Germany, also known as "Schloss Glücksburg."

APPEARANCE: Upright, compact, up to 4 ft (1.2 m) tall and 35 in (90 cm) wide.

FLOWERS: The color of the cupped flowers changes in the course of the blooming period. They are initially apricot changing in full bloom to an amber yellow with white towards the edges. They are very big, rosette-shaped and full, with diameters of 3 in (9 cm), and emit a delicate rose fragrance.

SPECIAL QUALITIES: A robust English Rose with healthy leaves blooming all summer long without break. Hardly any other variety shows such regular, symmetrical flowers.

USAGE: This variety is suitable as a bed rose or a potted plant thanks to its short, compact appearance.

SIMILAR VARIETIES: "Pegasus" also smells like Tea Roses. The bright yellow flowers, which lighten towards the edges, resemble Japanese Roses (about 3 ft/1 m tall and wide).

"Gertrude Jekyll" Rose

ORIGIN: Cultivation, Austin 1987.

APPEARANCE: Upright, bushy, quick-growing, 4 ft (1.2 m) tall and 35 in (90 cm) wide.

FLOWERS: The deep pink flowers are densely packed. You can hardly believe that they grow on such small, charming stems. They create a perfect harmony with the gray-green leaves and their fragrance is intense.

Location:
☼

Qualities:
❀❀❀ ♪

Usage:
🗑 ↕ ✗

SPECIAL QUALITIES: This variety will fill you with nostalgia because, while the large, rosette-shaped flowers have the charm of Portland Roses, the peaky leaves resemble Damask Roses. Resulting from a mix of the "Wife of Bath" and the old Portland Rose, "Comte de Chambord," the rose got its name in honor of British garden writer Getrude Jekyll.

USAGE: It is recommended for groups of 2 – 3 plants. The leaves are used to produce perfume because of their high rose oil content.

SIMILAR VARIETIES: "The Countryman" blooms with rosette-shaped, deep rose-pink flowers with a tender scent reminiscent of Old Roses.

"Golden Celebration" Rose

ORIGIN: Cultivation, Austin 1992.

APPEARANCE: Bushy shrub, overhanging branches, 4 ft (1.2 m) wide and tall.

FLOWERS: The unusual golden to coppery yellow flowers catch the eye immediately. When you go near the flowers, you will see that the color consists of many small, pink points. Dense, full flowers are very large, with diameters of 5 in (12 cm). They give off a pleasant fragrance.

SPECIAL QUALITIES: This elegant rose with huge golden-yellow flowers is a hybrid of the well-known English Roses, "Charles Austin" and "Graham Thomas." It is highly resistant to diseases.

USAGE: This well-formed, round shrub with elegantly hanging branches looks good individually or in groups. It is also suitable as a potted plant or available as a tree.

SIMILAR VARIETIES: The dark yellow, wide, cupped flowers of "Teasing Georgia" get lighter towards the edges.

"Graham Thomas" Rose

ORIGIN: Cultivation, Austin 1983.

APPEARANCE: Bushy shrub, many branches, quickly growing, overhanging, 4 – 5 ft (1.20 – 1.50 m) tall, 3 – 4 ft
(1 – 1.20 m) wide.

FLOWERS: The strong, full flowers are pure yellow and are
permeated by a pleasant Tea Rose fragrance. This variety
blooms several times a season, but also has a long main
blooming period.

SPECIAL QUALITIES: This robust variety is beloved for more
than its pure yellow flowers. It also grows excellently in
colder climates and is ideal for beginner rose cultivators. It
sometimes grows very quickly in warmer regions.
You should prune the long shoots.

USAGE: This rose looks nice in beds because of its
bushy character. Up to 3 plants form a luxurious group.
It grows in hot, sunny locations as well as in half-shade.
As a potted plant, "Graham Thomas" decorates any
patio and balcony beautifully. Moreover, the variety is
available as a tree that reaches 4 ft (1.2 m) in height. It
provides nice cut flowers for a vase.

Location:
☼ – ☀

Qualities:
✿✿ ✍

Usage:
🏺 🌱 ✂ ✗

"Heritage" Rose

Location:

☼

Qualities:

Usage:
🗑 🖊 ✂ ✗

ORIGIN: Cultivation, Austin 1984.

APPEARANCE: Bushy shrub, round, regularly branched, quick growing, overhanging branches and few thorns, 3 – 5 ft (1 – 1.5 m) tall.

FLOWERS: The strong, full flowers charm you with their tender, porcelain pink hue. Moreover, they have a very pleasant fragrance, bringing to mind a mix of honey and fruit. They bloom in dense clusters early in summer and again in the fall. The weak leaves resemble those of Musk Roses and perfectly complement the warm color of the flowers.

SPECIAL QUALITIES: This variety is one of the most popular English Roses. No wonder, since the sporty flowers are full in shape. The shrub grows quickly and continuously forms new shoots, so the lovely flowers do not stop blooming.

USAGE: This shapely shrub looks equally pretty individually or in a group. It is also recommended as a potted plant and or as a tree. Its pretty, fragrant flowers are ideal for cutting and rose recipes.

COMPANIONS IN ROMANTIC FLOWER BUNCHES

You can arrange English Roses not only in your garden, but also in bouquets with other flowers. But they should complement each other in shape and color and the tender romantic character of English Roses should be emphasized. The blue tones of bellflowers, catmint, lavender, larkspur, blue violet or other plants match pink and red hues especially well. Roses in the yellow to apricot spectrum go well with white flowers, e.g., with asters, lilies, feather pinks, dogwood or baby's breath. Mixing the yellow flowers with green plants with decorative leaves or using color-contrasting arrangements will create a charming picture.

"Jayne Austin" Rose

ORIGIN: Cultivation, Austin 1990.

APPEARANCE: Bushy shrub, upright, quick growing, many new shoots always grow from the base, 4 ft (1.2 m) tall and 35 in (90 cm) wide.

FLOWERS: The large, rosette-shaped flowers bloom in a warm apricot-yellow color. They grow in dense clusters and have an intense fragrance like Tea Roses. As for color, they harmonize with the light-green leaves and are certain to bloom repeatedly.

SPECIAL QUALITIES: This charming variety, with its velvety, glossy flowers, resembles the old, climbing "Gloire de Dijon" rose. It tends to form long, climbing shoots that you should prune to achieve a shrub-like appearance.

USAGE: This bushy, small Shrub Rose is recommended for planting on large areas as well as in hedges. It grows well as a potted plant and provides nice, pleasantly scented cut flowers.

SIMILAR VARIETIES: "Charity" has even bigger, but at the same time more delicate, flowers than "Jayne Austin." Their intense fragrance is reminiscent of myrtle.

"Leander" Rose

ORIGIN: Cultivation, Austin 1982.

APPEARANCE: Wide bushy shrub, upright, quick growing, 6 ft (1.8 m) tall and 5 ft (1.5 m) wide.

FLOWERS: Densely packed flowers shine with an apricot hue, a bit darker in the center. They resemble the Gallica Rose, "Charles de Mills," with their elegant shape. They bloom in big clusters and contrast with the deep-green leaves. They have a strong, fruity fragrance. The main blooming period is in early summer, in later summer a second, weaker blooming period follows.

SPECIAL QUALITIES: "Leander" is characterized by healthy leaves absolutely resistant to rose diseases. It is very similar to its parent, "Charles Austin," but its fine flowers are smaller and at the same time shaped perfectly symmetrically.

USAGE: This luxurious shrub can be planted either individually or in groups. It is suitable for beds and larger areas. Lots of plants need lots of space, however. It complements other big shrubs well. The nice potted plant is also available as a tree.

Location:
☼

Qualities:
❀❀❀ ♪

Usage:
🧺 ‡ ✕

"Mary Rose" Rose

ORIGIN: Cultivation, Austin 1983.

APPEARANCE: Bushy, well branched, upright, not too strong, but regularly growing, 3 – 4 ft (1 – 1.20 m) tall and wide.

FLOWERS: Densely packed, the medium-sized flowers are bright pink with dark centers. They look like Old Roses and have the same tender fragrance. They complement their medium-green, glossy leaves perfectly.

SPECIAL QUALITIES: The blooming period starts in early summer and ends late. Another blooming period soon follows since this rose blooms almost continuously. The flowers resist rain well and the plant itself is not susceptible to rose diseases.

USAGE: The shrub is already very decorative alone, but it is even more impressive in a small group. 2 – 3 plants are best for 1 square yard/meter. The rose grows well even on sunny, hot locations. It is attractive as a potted plant for a patio or a balcony. As a tree, it is very impressive as well. Cut roses are long-lasting.

Similar varieties: The deep pink-blooming "Portmeiron" grows 35 in (90 cm) tall and wide and looks good in every garden.

IF ENGLISH ROSES STAND IN RAIN

The luxurious flower balls of English Roses look nice, but if they soak up water during rain they become unbelievably heavy. The flower shoots bend under this weight on shrubs with overhanging branches. In a rainy place, bushy upright varieties such as "Mary Rose" are more suitable. Varieties with this appearance are also recommended for pond banks. You simply let several branches hang and they are reflected in the water.

"Othello" Rose

ORIGIN: Cultivation, Austin 1986.

APPEARANCE: Bushy shrub, upright, dense, shoots have few thorns, 3 – 4 ft (1 – 1.2 m) tall and about 35 in (90 cm) wide.

FLOWERS: Flowers are a dark crimson that becomes purple when wilting. They are dense and full and the outer petals roll decoratively outwards. They are very big, with diameters of 5 – 5½ in (12 – 14 cm), and they have the strong fragrance of Old Roses. This variety blooms late, but almost continuously.

SPECIAL QUALITIES: The deep red flowers also come in cherry red to mauve tones. They look very regal above the dark-green leaves. A bit susceptible to powdery mildew, unfortunately.

USAGE: "Othello" is suitable as an individual plant, but it works even more effectively in small groups for beds or hedges. 1 – 2 plants are recommended for each square yard/meter. Because this rose does not grow very big, it is a good choice for gardens and pots. The Baroque blossoms are good in bouquets and arrangements and they should be used in rose recipes because of their unusual color and fragrance.

Decorate with Rose Petals

You can decorate writing paper, turn tea lamps or chimney lamps into warm light shades and much more with dried petals. Pick roses in full bloom early in the morning after the dew has dried. Clean the individual petals, put them on a kitchen paper and dry 1 – 2 hours. And in the end, put silica gel into a pot and cover with an air-tight lid. You can also use detergent powder. Distribute the petals loosely on this film and put more gel on them. Repeat for layers. Let the covered pot sit for 5 – 7 days and when petals are dry you can start to glue.

"Pretty Jessica" Rose

Location:

Qualities:

Usage:

ORIGIN: Cultivation, Austin 1983.

APPEARANCE: Bushy, low, compact, about 30 in (75 cm) tall and 24 in (60 cm) wide.

FLOWERS: Densely packed flowers shine a warm pink resembling Pale Roses. They first open cup-shaped and then effloresce in dense rosettes. They appear continuously all summer and spread an intense fragrance. They contrast nicely with the medium-green leaves.

SPECIAL QUALITIES: The offspring of "Wife of Bath" is beloved for its old-fashioned charm reminiscent of Old Roses and for its compact appearance. The leaves are slightly susceptible to rose diseases. The best prevention is, as in other cases, to choose a location suitable for roses.

USAGE: This small rose does not need much space and thus it is also recommended for small gardens. It best decorates beds in small groups of 3 – 5. It is at home in a pot on a patio or balcony and provides nice cut roses.

SIMILAR VARIETIES: The dark red "Prospero" is also suitable for small gardens, as is the apricot-colored "Tamora."

THEY ARE STRONG TOGETHER

A small group of roses lends your garden a romantic charm
because it is more striking – not counting potted plants –
than an individual. If you keep a distance of 20 in (50 cm)
between individual plants in the group – proportionally
more for bigger varieties – plants grow to be dense, shapely
shrubs.

"Redouté" Rose

Location:

☼

Qualities:
❀❀❀ 〜

Usage:
🪣 ⚘ ✂

ORIGIN: Cultivation, Austin 1992.

APPEARANCE: Bushy, well branched, upright, not too strong, but regularly growing, about 4 ft (1.2 m) tall and wide.

FLOWERS: The densely packed, medium-sized flowers are a tender pink and the outer petals are almost white. They look like old Alba Roses and have the same delicate fragrance. They harmonize perfectly with their medium-green, glossy leaves.

SPECIAL QUALITIES: This variety – named after the famous painter of roses – is an offspring of the pink-red flowering "Mary Rose." They are hardly distinguishable except for the color of the flowers. They also bloom early and almost continuously until the end of summer. The flowers are rain-resistant and the leaves very healthy.

USAGE: This Bed Rose is perfect either individually or in small groups. 2 – 3 plants are ideal for 1 square yard/meter. It also tolerates sunny and hot locations. Trees are especially eye-catching in pots as well as in beds. Nice cut roses last a long time in a vase.

"Scepter d'Isle" Rose

ORIGIN: Cultivation, Austin 1996.

APPEARANCE: Upright, slender, 35 in (90 cm) tall and up to 30 in (75 cm) wide.

FLOWERS: The tender pink flowers are relatively small, but they bloom luxuriantly. They open like cups, showing their yellow anthers in the middle. Myrtle fragrance is typical of English Roses and resembles that of "Constance Spry."

Location:
☼

Qualities:
❀❀ ♪

Usage:
🏺 ✂ ✗

SPECIAL QUALITIES: This continuously blooming variety has bounteous, pure pink flowers above dark-green leaves.

USAGE: This tall rose is suitable for flower and border beds where it looks best in small groups. 2 – 3 plants quickly form a thick bush. It is stunning as a tree or in a pot – with a stalk height of 4 ft (1.2 m) and a bushy crown. Moreover, it provides nice, long-lasting cut roses.

SIMILAR VARITIES: The tender pink and white "St. Swithun" is recommended to lovers of myrrh fragrance.

"Shropshire Lass" Rose

ORIGIN: Cultivation, Austin 1968

APPEARANCE: Upright, quick growing, up to 8 ft (2.5 m) tall
and 6 ft (1.8 m) wide, even taller in warmer regions.

FLOWERS: Its big, half-full flowers are tender pink, fading
over time to almost white. They open cup-shaped, revealing golden-yellow anthers. They have a tender fragrance.
This variety blooms once in early summer.

SPECIAL QUALITIES: An unusual hybrid of the pink-blooming Tea Hybrid "Mme Butterfly" and the lemon-yellow
flowers *of rosa x alba*, or "Mme Legras de St. Germain."
You will recognize its similarity to Alba Roses. This variety
is hardy, not too susceptible to diseases and certain to
bloom lavishly.

USAGE: You can use this tall rose as a shrub as well as
a climber. We recommend that you plant it in groups of
two and more so that it fills in your bed. It creates a nice,
natural-looking hedge if you plant it in rows. The variety
also grows near woods and in nutrient-deficient soil.

Similar varieties: "Constance Spry" (see above) and "Snow Gloss" are also once-blooming and can be used in shrubs or as climbers. "Snow Gloss" – with its small, pure white, full flowers – nicely complements pink-blooming varieties.

IS IT NECESSARY TO PRUNE ONCE-BLOOMING ROSES?

Once-blooming varieties are normally not cut because they form their flowers on last year's shoots. You can prune wilted side shoots of older plants to 2-3 buds, but leave this year's shoots alone. This is recommended with "Shropshire Lass" because otherwise it only blooms on the top of old shoots and lacks visual appeal.

"The Dark Lady" Rose

Location:

Qualities:

Usage:

ORIGIN: Cultivation, Austin 1991. It is also known as "Dark Lady".

APPEARANCE: Upright, wide shrub, 35 in (90 cm tall), 35 – 43 in (90 – 110 cm) wide.

FLOWERS: The dense, full, dark-crimson flowers resemble peonies. They are very big, but loosely packed at the same time and the petals roll back a bit. It gives off a strong fragrance. The dark-green leaves contrast perfectly with the red flowers. This variety blooms many times a season.

SPECIAL QUALITIES: The offspring of the rose-red flowering "Mary Rose" and the red "Prospero" charms you with its warm, red flowers. It resembles "Mary Rose" in appearance and flower shape.

USAGE: This wide-growing, low shrub is suitable for larger surfaces. It also complements loose hedges well. It is best planted in small groups, where three can quickly grow into a thick shrub. This variety grows in bigger planters and pots well and is also available as a tree of 4 ft (1.2 m).

SIMILAR VARIETIES: "Falstaff" is characterized by its dense, full flowers of the deepest crimson which later turn purple. Moreover, it has a strong fragrance. The plant grows about 3 ft (1 m) tall and wide. The flowers of "Tess of the d'Urbervilles" also glow crimson and spread an intense fragrance. This variety grows compact, 35 in (90 cm) tall and 24 in (60 cm) wide, with elegant hanging branches.

STUNNING RED

Bright red flowers bring life to a garden, a patio or a balcony. They require a good choice of neighbors, however. The strong red looks lovely with soft pinks as well as with all violet and mauve hues while white and yellow stand in a sharp contrast.

"The Pilgrim" Rose

ORIGIN: Cultivation, Austin 1991. It is called "Gartenarchitekt Günther Schulze" in Germany.

APPEARANCE: Bushy shrub, upright, quickly growing, 3½ ft (1.1 m) tall and wide.

FLOWERS: The dense, full flowers are composed of many velvety yellow petals which are nearly white on the outer edges. The flowers open flat in a rosette shape and spread a strong fragrance. Glossy green leaves create a vivid display.

SPECIAL QUALITIES: A hybrid of the well-known varieties "Graham Thomas" and "Yellow Button:" healthy, robust and continuously blooming. It was the first variety to enrich the Romantic Rose family with yellow.

USAGE: In groups, suitable for beds or in rows for loose hedges. Individually, its compact appearance makes it an excellent potted plant. You can successfully combine its tender yellow flowers with other colors. Linear forms, such as mullein or montbrecia, complement the round flowers especially well.

"The Prince" Rose

ORIGIN: Cultivation, Austin 1990.

APPEARANCE: Low, bushy, about 30 in (75 cm tall) and 24 – 35 in (60 – 90 cm) wide, depending on plant density.

FLOWERS: The full flowers are deep-crimson first and gradually turn a shiny purple. They are cup-shaped, opening into a big, symmetrical rosette and often show a green eye. They look very smart over the deep-green leaves. The heavy fragrance of Old Roses fits them.

SPECIAL QUALITIES: A continuous bloomer with an unusual color. The strong crimson resembles the flowers of old Gallica Roses.

Location:
☼

Qualities:
❀❀ ↝

Usage:
🗑 ✂ ✗

USAGE: This compact rose is especially nice in small groups. It goes well with flower and border beds and loose hedges. As a potted plant, it enjoys balconies and patios. It provides nice cut roses.

ENHANCING A GARDEN WITH SMALL ROSES
Low roses – such as "The Prince" – are especially suitable for border beds or paths.

"Wife of Bath" Rose

Location:

Qualities:

Usage:

ORIGIN: Cultivation, Austin 1969.

APPEARANCE: Bushy shrub, well-branched but compact, hanging branches, 32 – 40 in (80 – 100 cm) tall and 24 in (60 cm) wide.

FLOWERS: The petals are full of color contrasts. While their inner surface shines a dark-pink, the outside is lighter. The cup-shaped flowers are half-full and have a myrtle fragrance. They grow above small, medium-green leaves and appear continuously throughout the season.

SPECIAL QUALITIES: An ideal rose for small gardens or as a potted plant because of its compact appearance. It is very robust in spite of its small size. Dead shoots must removed and they grow back very quickly.

USAGE: This rose can be planted separately, but is more effective in groups of 3 – 5. One or two plants are enough for 1 square yard/meter. It goes well with flower and border beds and loose hedges. It is recommended as a potted plant and a cut rose.

SIMILAR VARIETIES: "Cottage Garden" – with its shiny pink, rosette-shaped flowers – is suitable, if you lack space for planting flowers.

"Winchester Cathedral" Rose

ORIGIN: Cultivation, Austin 1988.

APPEARANCE: Bushy shrub, 4 ft (1.2 m) tall and wide.

FLOWERS: Dense, full, white flowers with a tender fragrance. They are sometimes yellow in the center in late summer. This rose blooms almost continually in a nice summer.

SPECIAL QUALITIES: "Winchester Cathedral" is one of the nicest white English Roses. This variety is a sport – i.e., a spontaneous hybrid – of the pink-red "Mary Rose" and it is very similar to it, except for the color of the flowers.

USAGE: This decorative shrub is an eye-catcher individually as well as in groups in the garden. With its white flowers and mixed with woody plants, it contrasts with and cheers up dark plots. It is suitable as a potted plant and also available as a tree.

SIMILAR VARIETIES: "Glamis Castle" has similar, beautiful, white flowers and a strong myrrh fragrance. It is significantly smaller, with a height of 35 in (90 cm), and is ideal for small gardens and pots.

Location:
☼

Qualities:
❀❀ ჟ

Usage:
🪴 🌳

GREAT GROUND COVERS

This group includes all robust and low-maintenance rose varieties that make large surfaces green quickly and painlessly. We cannot imagine public parks without them and they are also increasingly popular in private gardens. Hardly any other rose group is as multi-functional as this one. Their appearance ranges from flat-growing, tightly ground-hugging plants to upright bushes with partly hanging branches. Most of them are low and bushy. Small Shrub Roses are a good alternative to big Shrub Roses in small gardens.

The color spectrum covers mainly pink tones, but there are also white, red and yellow varieties. You can mix them well with each other and with perennials planted in the open spaces among roses or on the border. Dark colors, such as blues or violets, create the strongest contrast.

Even though Ground Covers seem indestructible, you should pay attention to several factors. Their location must be sunny and the soil carefully weeded. Spreading bark mulch among the plants will save you a lot of weeding. The mulch is needed only until a dense plant cover has been created. True-rooted varieties are especially robust. They multiply by means of root suckers (i.e., are not cultivated) and need not be covered with soil for winter. You must rejuvenate Ground Covers every four to five years and prune them back about 12 in (30 cm).

"Aspirin" Rose

ORIGIN: Cultivation, Tantau 1997.

APPEARANCE: Wide bushy shrub, 24 – 32 in (60 – 80 cm) tall, 16 in (40 cm) wide (class 3 bellow).

FLOWERS: A Floribunda Rose with white, full, continuously blooming flowers. They grow in dense clusters and nearly overwhelem the light-green leaves. If it is cold, the flowers are tinted with a tender pink.

SPECIAL QUALITIES: This robust and low-maintenance rose blooms continuously throughout the whole summer. You can use it as a Ground Cover or a Bed Rose. It was awarded an ADR premium in 1995.

USAGE: This rose is multi-functional. It is a nice individual shrub and also grows well in a pot. It is available as a decorative tree as well. It looks terrific from a distance in groups and is suitable for stabilizing hillsides. The flowers are rain-resistant and enjoy moister areas. Moreover, this variety is very heat-resistant and is suitable for hot, sunny places as well as for half-shade.

GROUND COVERS ARE SUB-DIVIDED ACCORDING TO THEIR APPEARANCE

Group 1: lying on the ground, slowly growing, space needed 3 – 4 per square yard/meter.
Group 2: upright growing, 2 – 3 plants per square yard/meter according to the usage.
Group 3: low, bushy, according to the desired density 2 or 3 – 4 plants per square yard/meter.
Group 4: rather upright, tall, with slightly bent, hanging branches, the distance between individual plants is usually half their height.
Group 5: lying, but quickly growing, distance among the plants is calculated according to the shoot length and how quickly a plant carpet is created.

"Ballerina" Rose

Location:
☼ – ☀

Qualities:
✿✿✿ ✾

Usage:
🪴 🌱

ORIGIN: Cultivation. Bentall 1937.

APPEARANCE: Upright up to hanging, densely branched, 28 – 35 in (70 – 90 cm) tall and wide (group 4 above).

FLOWERS: The simple, crimson-pink flowers with white central eyes create big floral clusters. They bend under the load like a bow. They bloom again after the first, luxurious bloom.

SPECIAL QUALITIES: The offspring of Musk Roses has many positive qualities. Nature lovers love them because the continuously appearing flowers are a favored nectar source for bees and bumble-bees.

FRUIT: Many hips.

USAGE: This rose is an eye-catcher standing alone or in groups. It matches loose hedges, stabilizes hillsides and grows in half-shade as well as in full sun. Because it is very easy to care for, it is good for planting on graves. 2 – 3 plants are recommended for 1 square yard/meter to cover the ground. It looks very decorative in a pot or as a tree.

"Fair Play" Rose

ORIGIN: Cultivation, Ilsing/Interplant 1977.

APPEARANCE: Wide bushy shrub, long and hanging branches, 3 – 5 ft (1 – 1.5 m) tall and 32 – 40 in (80 – 100 cm) wide (group 4 above).

FLOWERS: Light red with a white center and clearly visible yellow anthers. Flowers are half-full and open like cups. Their diameter is about 3 in (7 cm). Individual flowers grow in dense clusters that contrast in color with the matte, dark-green leaves.

SPECIAL QUALITIES: A small, robust, low-maintenance Shrub Rose.

USAGE: A good choice for larger surfaces because it grows well and is low-maintenance. It reinforces hillsides and dams and is also very pretty in a bed among other small Shrub Roses.

SIMILAR VARIETIES: "Rosy Carpet," a variety by the same cultivator, is very similar. It grows as a wide shrub, but is compact and reaches 4 ft (1.2 m) tall. The simple, cup-shaped flowers are vivid crimson-pink with white centers and possess a fragrance similar to Wild Roses.

Location:
☼

Qualities:
❀❀

"Fleurette" Rose

Location:
☼

Qualities:

ORIGIN: Cultivation, Ilsing/Interplant 1977.

APPEARANCE: Upright with overhanging branches, wide growing and strongly branched, 3 – 4 ft (1 – 1.2 m) tall and 4 – 5 ft (1.2 – 1.4 m) wide (group 4 above).

FLOWERS: The simple, cup-shaped flowers consist of five petals that are shiny pink outside with crimson rims and white insides. They are 1 – 2 in (3 – 5 cm) wide, and 10 – 12 of them appear in loose clusters. The flowers have a tender fragrance.

FRUIT: Many hips.

SPECIAL QUALITIES: A robust, weather-resistant and amply blooming variety, very low-maintenance and quick-growing.

USAGE: This plentifully blooming rose, shaped like a Shrub Rose, is suitable for greening larger surfaces and hillsides. It matches hedges and beds and may be combined with perennials. It looks especially good with a backdrop of woody plants. 1 – 2 plants can fill 1 square yard/meter, depending on their density.

"Gärtnerfreude" Rose

ORIGIN: Cultivation, Kordes 1999.

APPEARANCE: Low, compact wide shrub, 20 in (50 cm) tall and wide (group 3 above).

FLOWERS: The small, dense, full flowers are raspberry-red. They grow in umbels and keep their color until wilting.

SPECIAL QUALITIES: The variety is appropriately named. It belongs to the group of the especially robust Rigo® Roses and is very weather-resistant. It is, therefore, recommended for rainy regions. This attractive rose was awarded an ADR premium in addition to other prizes in 2001.

USAGE: It quickly makes bare surfaces green and is beloved in a private garden as well as in public places. 3 – 4 plants per square yard/meter create a dense floral carpet. This variety is also suitable as a potted plant and available as a tree.

SIMILAR VARIETIES: "Mainaufeuer" blooms continuously with blood-red, full flowers. The plant is 20 in (50 cm) tall and grows as a dense carpet.

Location:
☼

Qualities:
❀❀❀

Usage:
🪴 ⚘

"Gelbe Dagmar Hastrop" Rose

Location:

☼ – ☀

Qualities:

ORIGIN: Cultivation, Moore 1989. An offspring of the Ramanas Rose.

APPEARANCE: Upright, 24 – 32 in (60 – 80 cm) tall and wide (group 2 above).

FLOWERS: The yellow, half-full flowers grow individually or in clusters and spread a pleasant fragrance. The variety blooms again after the main blooming period in summer.

FRUIT: Many big hips of about 1 in (2.5 cm) in diameter.

SPECIAL QUALITIES: Frost-resistant as well as salt-resistant, true-rooted Ground Covers. They are beloved by bees and bumble-bees for shedding lots of pollen. They have a nice autumn yellow shade on their leaves.

USAGE: You can plant the rose individually or in groups, on plains and hillsides or in hedges as well as on patios or graves. It also tolerates half-shade.

SIMILAR VARIETIES: "Dagmar Hastrup" blooms with simple, pink flowers and gives off a soft fragrance. It grows upright, 24 – 40 in (60 – 100 cm) tall according to plant density.

THE MOST ROBUST

The offspring of Ramanas Roses (*rosa rugosa*) are not susceptible to diseases and are very frost-resistant. True-rooted varieties are moreover salt-resistant. They have many things to offer: They have nice, simple to loosely-packed flowers, spread a very pleasant fragrance and their leaves turn yellow when winter starts. They show many big hips at the same time. They are food for bees and provide a shelter for small animals all year long. The flowers are sensitive to rain and cold. You should prune them each year to prevent them from becoming too bushy.

"Heidekönigin" Rose

Location:
☼ – ☀

Qualities:
❀❀❀ ↶

Usage:
🪴 ⚱

ORIGIN: Cultivation, Kordes 1985.

APPEARANCE: Ground Cover, up to 6 ft (2 m) long, bent shoots, about 20 in (50 cm) tall (group 5 above).

FLOWERS: The dense, full, pure pink flowers open in the center in efflorescence. They grow to 3 in (8 cm) wide and have a tender fragrance similar to that of Wild Roses. The finely branched shoots have luxurious flower umbels and are mostly hanging.

SPECIAL QUALITIES: This variety is more suitable for larger surfaces than for small gardens because of its quick growth. Bent shoots and many flowers look really good.

USAGE: A luxurious Ground Cover suitable for greening larger surfaces. You can fix long shoots on supporting structures and let them grow to the sky. The variety is also available as a tree.

SIMILAR VARIETIES: "Immense" (simple, pearl-pink, once-blooming flowers) and "Marondo" (shiny pink, half-full) also grow very quickly and may be also used as climbers.

"Heidetraum" Rose

ORIGIN: Cultivation, Noack 1988.

APPEARANCE: Wide shrub, overhanging, up to 4 ft (1.2 m) long branches, 28 – 32 in (70 – 80 cm) tall (group 3 above).

FLOWERS: The half-full flowers shine a strong crimson. Up to 25 blossoms create big umbels which cover the dense leaves for many months.

SPECIAL QUALITIES: Like all varieties of the flower-carpet type, "Heidetraum" is not susceptible to powdery mildew or black spots. This variety was awarded an ADR premium in 1990.

USAGE: This small Shrub Rose is a robust, low-maintenance Ground Cover. 3 plants per square yard/ meter make a dense floral carpet suitable for hillsides and graves.

SIMILAR VARIETIES: Other varieties: "Alcantara" (dark-red), "Celina" (yellow), "Heidefeuer" (shiny red), "Medusa" (lavender-pink and full) and "Schnee-flocke" (pure white).

Location:
☼

Qualities:
❀❀❀

Usage:
▦ ⚘

"Lavender Dream" Rose

Location:
☼

Qualities:
❀❀🎵

Usage:
🪣

ORIGIN: Cultivation, Interplant 1985.

APPEARANCE: First an upright bush, then a wide shrub. Branches bend under the mass of flowers, 24 – 40 in (60 – 100 cm) tall (group 4 above).

FLOWERS: Lavender-colored, loose, full flowers, with a sweet fragrance, develop from round, red buds. They open cup-shaped and reach a diameter of about 2 in (5 cm). Yellow anthers are clearly visible in this state. The luxurious umbels consist of many blossoms.

SPECIAL QUALITIES: This true-rooted variety was awarded an ADR premium in 1987 thanks to its unusual floral color and robust appearance.

USAGE: This early blooming, low-maintenance, small Shrub Rose is suitable on its own or in groups for greening larger garden plots. It is also recommended for hillsides. 2 – 3 plants are enough to cover one square yard/meter. This variety can be combined with perennials and small woody plants. It tolerates hot southern exposures and is also suitable for roof gardens.

"Lovely Fairy" Rose

ORIGIN: Cultivation, Vurens / Spek 1992.

APPEARANCE: Low, bushy branched, wide growing, 24 – 32 in (60 – 80 cm) tall and wide (group 3 above).

FLOWERS: The full flowers are strongly pink at first and open like a cup later, turning lighter and showing a white center. The individual flowers are small, with diameters of ½ – 1 in (2 – 2.5 cm), and many of them grow in umbels.

SPECIAL QUALITIES: A hybrid of the well-known Ground Cover, "The Fairy," similar to the mother plant in its appearance and qualities, but even more lusciously bloom- ing. It is very tolerant of hot locations, but also rain- resistant and needs almost no care.

USAGE: Useful individually or in groups, in sunny locations and in half-shade. 3 – 4 plants are enough to create a dense floral carpet over 1 square yard/meter. These true-rooted plants can be part of a heather garden and are recommended for hillsides and roof gardens. The variety is also suitable as a Miniature, half-tree, tree or as a potted plant.

Location:
☼ – ☀

Qualities:
❀❀❀

Usage:
🪴 🌱

"Magic Meidiland" Rose

Location:
☼

Qualities:

USAGE: Cultivation, Meilland / KBN Strobel 1992.

ORIGIN: Flat shrub, shoots up to 4 ft (1.2 m), planted together 16 – 20 in (40 – 50 cm) tall (group 5 above).

APPEARANCE: Vividly pink, strong, full flowers that open like cups. Their diameter is about 1½ in (4 cm). A stem carries up to 15 blossoms.

FLOWERS: This robust Ground Cover was awarded an ADR premium in 1995. It is characterized by its high resistance to powdery mildew and black spots.

SPECIAL QUALITIES: A robust, frost-resistant Ground Cover which also tolerates air-polluted locations near roads. It grows very quickly and needs almost no care.

USAGE: The French cultivator Meilland created a spectacular spectrum of Ground Covers called the Meidiland Group. They bloom continuously and are frost-resistant, rain-resistant and heat-tolerant. You can find a selection of them bellow:

THE MEIDILAND FAMILY

"Alba Meidiland": Dense, full, white flowers; bushy; 32 – 40 in (80 – 100 cm) tall.

"Bingo Meidiland": Simple, pink flowers; bushy; 16 – 24 in (40 – 60 cm) tall; ADR predicate in 1994.

"Colossal Meidiland": Big, dark-red, full flowers, upright, bushy, 24 – 40 in (60 – 80 cm) tall.

"Lovely Meidiland": Light pink, strong, full flowers; bushy; 16 – 20 in (40 – 50 cm) tall.

"Phlox Meidiland": Simple, pink flowers with light centers, similar to Wild Roses; shrubs; 24 – 40 in (60 – 80 cm) tall.

"Pink Meidiland": Simple, pink-white flowers; 24 – 40 in (60 – 80 cm) tall with overhanging branches.

"Red Meidiland": Simple, red, cupped flowers; low and bushy growing; 16 – 20 in (40 – 50 cm) tall.

"Max Graf" Rose

ORIGIN: Cultivation, Bowditsch 1919. Probable parents are *rosa rugosa x rosa wichuraiana.*

APPEARANCE: Wide, bushy; quick-growing; partly lying, partly bent, 3 – 10 ft (1 – 3 m) long shoots. The plant carpet is 12 – 16 in (30 – 40 cm) tall with large spaces between the individual plants; if denser, the roses reach together 20 – 24 in (50 – 60 cm) (group 5 above).

FLOWERS: Pink, simple, cupped flowers of 1½ – 2½ in (4 – 6 cm) in diameter. They grow individually or in small clusters above glossy, dark-green leaves. The petals fade in full blossom. Buds are crimson. The blooming period last through June.

SPECIAL QUALITIES: A quick-growing, once-blooming Ground Cover, also suitable for extreme locations. Very frost-resistant.

USAGE: This variety is a good choice for anyone who wants low, dense floral carpets. It is suitable for big, flat plots as well as for hillsides. 1 – 2 plants are ample for 1 square yard/meter.

NATURAL EROSION-PROTECTION WITH GROUND COVERS

Growing on hillsides is often problematic. However, by using Ground Covers, you can cultivate a useful and beautiful hillside garden. The long, low shoots of Ground Covers create firm, new roots and there is no better erosion-protection. The dense plant carpet protects soil from weeds as well. True-rooted varieties have many advantages: wild shoots need not be removed and a winter soil cover is not necessary. The varieties of group 5 above are suitable for larger surfaces, such as "Max Graf," "Rote Max Graf" or "Weisse Max Graf."

"Mozart" Rose

Location:
☼

Qualities:

ORIGIN: Cultivation, Lambert 1937.

APPEARANCE: Bushy shrub, upright, partly hanging shoots, 24 – 40 in (60 – 100 cm) tall according to plant density, and about 24 in (60 cm) wide (group 4 above).

FLOWERS: The simple, cupped flowers are crimson with light centers and shiny yellow anthers. They have a pleasing fragrance and are, with individual diameters of ½ – 1 in (2 – 3 cm), relatively small. But they bloom continuously in dense umbels.

SPECIAL QUALITIES: The sporty offspring of *rosa moschata* are similar to Wild Roses and have an old-fashioned charm. Although it is an older variety, it has not lost any of its popularity.

USAGE: A small Shrub Rose, suitable as a Ground Cover as well as alone. Some sellers also offer it as part of a group of decorative rose shrubs. Groups are planted at 3 – 4 per square yard/meter.

SIMILAR VARIETIES: "Cherry Meidiland" has simple, red flowers with white centers and grows bushy, 24 – 28 in (60 – 70 cm) tall.

"Palmengarten Frankfurt" Rose

ORIGIN: Cultivation, Kordes 1988.

APPEARANCE: Bushy to shrubby, partly with hanging branches, about 28 in (70 cm) tall and up to 3 ft (1 m) wide early in the second year (group 3 above).

FLOWERS: Vivid pink, dense, full flowers develop from drop-shaped, red buds. They are cup-shaped, 3 – 4 in (8 – 10 cm) in diameter and grow in dense umbels above glossy, green leaves. The pink flowers contrast with the fresh, green leaves.

SPECIAL QUALITIES: This small, but robust and low-maintenance Shrub Rose blooms amply until fall and was awarded an ADR premium in 1992.

USAGE: If you are looking for quick-growing, amply blooming Ground Covers, this is the right choice for you. 1 – 2 plants per square yard/meter suffice to create a dense floral carpet. This variety is also available as a tree or as a nice, decorative potted plant.

SIMILAR VARIETIES: "Mirato" is robust and low-maintenance. The half-full flowers are shiny pink.

Location:
☼

Qualities:
❀❀❀

Usage:
🪴 ↕

"Roseromantic" Rose

Location:

☼

Qualities:

✿✿ ❀ ⌣

ORIGIN: Cultivation, Kordes 1984.

APPEARANCE: Bushy shrub, wide, with overhanging, thin shoots, up to 24 in (60 cm) tall and wide (group 4 above).

FLOWERS: The simple flowers are tender pink at first, later fading to pinkish white. They consist of five egg-shaped, slightly wavy petals growing in dense umbels. The yellow anthers contrast with the pink petals. They give off a lovely fragrance.

SPECIAL QUALITIES: This variety is reminiscent of Wild Roses and blooms lavishly until fall.

USAGE: This rose gives a natural charm to larger areas and combines well with perennials and small woody plants. 5 – 6 plants per square yard/meter can be planted according to the density you wish. If you plant them densely, they mostly grow to be more than 24 in (60 cm) tall.

SIMILAR VARIETIES: The salmon-pink flowers of "Relax Meidiland," 20 – 40 in/50 – 60 cm, also have the charm of Wild Roses.

"Rote Max Graf" Rose

ORIGIN: Cultivation, Kordes 1980.

APPEARANCE: Lying, quickly growing shoots, 3 – 6 ft (1 – 2 m) long and about 20 in (50 cm) tall, 35 in (90 cm) tall if planted densely (group 5 above).

FLOWERS: The shiny red, velvety flowers with white centers are composed of wavy petals. They keep their color for a long time and grow in small clusters above contrasting, dark-green leaves.

FRUIT: Many hips.

SPECIAL QUALITIES: A low-maintenance, self-cleaning Ground Cover that quickly creates dense carpets. It is known for its frost-resistance.

USAGE: This variety greens large areas in private and public gardens and is suitable for reinforcing hillsides. 1 plant is enough for 1 square yard/meter because it grows extremely quickly.

SIMILAR VARIETIES: The simple, cupped, blindingly white flowers of "Weisse Max Graf" complement it ideally.

Location:
☼

Qualities:
❀ ⚘

"Sea Foam" Rose

Location:

Qualities:

Usage:

ORIGIN: Cultivation, E.W. Schwartz 1964.

APPEARANCE: Wide bush or shrub; compact, with bent, later lying shoots, up to 5 ft (1.5 m) long and 20 in (50 cm) tall (group 3 above).

FLOWERS: The white, full flowers have a tender pink touch at first and turn creamy white later. They appear in clusters and spread a weak fragrance. The leathery, glossy leaves make the color effect even stronger.

SPECIAL QUALITIES: This frost-resistant Shrub Rose charms you with its abundant flowers in a nostalgic round shape. It is named appropriately because its floral carpet spreads like sea foam.

USAGE: It quickly greens small as well as big areas. 3 – 4 plants per square yard/meter are recommended to create a dense carpet. With its hanging shoots, it is suitable for hanging pots and baskets.

SIMILAR VARIETIES: If you like densely packed flower balls, you will also like "White Bells," "Pink Bells," and "Red Bells."

"Sommerabend" Rose

ORIGIN: Cultivation, Kordes 1995.

APPEARANCE: Wide bush, but flat and quickly growing at the same time, shoots up to 4 ft (1.2 m) long and 12 in (30 cm) tall (group 5 above).

FLOWERS: The simple, cup-shaped flowers shine a dark red toned with a yellow center. They are medium-sized with diameters of 2 – 3 in (6 – 8 cm). They grow in luxurious clusters above glossy, green leaves. The blooming period lasts continuously until fall.

SPECIAL QUALITIES: A very healthy and heat-resistant rose with deep red, rain-proof flowers. It is also a beloved bee food and was awarded an ADR predicate in 1996.

USAGE: A densely growing Ground Cover that greens large areas quickly. You can plant it individually. If you plant in groups, 2 – 3 plants are recommended for 1 square yard/meter. The robust, true-rooted variety is also suitable for problematic locations and hillsides or roof gardens. It enjoys hanging pots or bigger planters and it is very nice as a tree.

Location:
☼

Qualities:
✿✿✿

Usage:

"Sommerwind" Rose

ORIGIN: Cultivation, Kordes 1985. Syn. "Surrey," "Vent d'Été."

APPEARANCE: Shrub to wide bush, with lying and hanging bent shoots, 20 – 28 in (50 – 70 cm) tall and up to 4 ft (1.2 m) wide (group 3 above).

FLOWERS: The cup-shaped, pink flowers develop from drop-shaped, pink-red buds. They are loosely packed, with beautiful, slightly wavy petals and diameters of about 1½ in (4 cm) each. The matte, glossy leaves are nearly covered with flowers all summer long. The flowers are very rain-resistant, but they wilt in the course of blooming.

SPECIAL QUALITIES: An unpretentious, robust, little Shrub Rose whose tender flowers give it an antiquated charm. It is a big-flowered counterpart of the well-known "Fairy" variety and was awarded an ADR predicate in 1987 along with other international prizes.

USAGE: This continuously blooming variety is suitable as a Ground Cover or as a Bed Rose. It grows in nearly any location, is frost-resistant and tolerates hot southern exposures as well as half-shade. It is not very vulnerable to

powdery mildew and black spots. It is also recommended for planting on graves and hillsides. It may be planted individually or in groups; 3 – 4 plants per square yard/meter create a dense floral carpet. It looks good in a pot or as a decorative tree. Because it is available as a tree with various stem-heights, it matches even the smallest balcony. Nature-lovers will love it because it attracts many bees and bumble-bees.

SIMILAR VARIETIES: "Sommermärchen" is a similar variety that originated in Kordes' cultivation as well. It blooms a strong pink and has a slight fragrance.

"Suma" Rose

Location:
☼

Qualities:
❀❀❀ ⟋

ORIGIN: Cultivation, Dr. Onodera 1989. Syn. "Harsuma".

APPEARANCE: Creeping, wide bush, shoots up to 5 ft (1.5 m) long, floral carpet about 20 in (50 cm) tall (group 5 above).

FLOWERS: The loosely packed, fragrant flowers range in color from ruby-red to dark-pink. Their light centers, with outstanding anthers, are eye-catching. They are cup-shaped and very beautiful with diameters of around 1 in (3 cm). Floral clusters appear along the shoots until fall and cover nearly the whole plant.

SPECIAL QUALITIES: This robust variety, originating in Japan, has been praised as one of the best by the Royal Horticultural Society. Its leaves are very decorative next to the beautiful flowers, especially when they turn crimson in the fall.

USAGE: If you like luxurious rose carpets, this variety is the right choice.

SIMILAR VARIETIES: "Royal Bassino" charms you with similarly beautiful flowers, but grows more compactly.

"Swany" Rose

ORIGIN: Cultivation, Meilland 1977. Syn. "Meiburenac."

APPEARANCE: Wide bushy shrub, quick growing, shoots partly lying, partly bent, up to 20 in (50 cm) tall and 20 – 24 in (50 – 60 cm) wide (group 3 above).

FLOWERS: The rosette-shaped, dense, white flowers give this rose a romantic charm. The flowers are ball-shaped at first and then open like a cup. They are 2 in (5 cm) wide on average and grow in big umbels. They harmonize with the glossy, green, feathery leaves.

SPECIAL QUALITIES: This richly and continuously blooming small Shrub Rose may be used in many ways, but is a bit susceptible to black spots. The shiny, white flowers are rain-resistant and cheer up dark corners.

USAGE: This variety can be planted individually or in groups of 3 – 4 plants per square yard/meter in a bed. It also enjoys locations less suitable for roses, reinforces hillsides, makes roof gardens green and grows well in pots, planters, and hanging pots. It is available as a tree with various stem heights.

Location:
☀

Qualities:
❀❀

Usage:

"The Fairy" Rose

Location:
☼ – ☀

Qualities:
❀❀

Usage:
🪴 🌱 ✂

ORIGIN: Cultivation, Bentall 1932.

APPEARANCE: Wide bush, partly hanging bent branches, 24 – 32 in (60 – 80 cm) tall, very often wider than its height (group 3 above).

FLOWERS: The small, rosette-shaped, full flowers are tender pink and very rain-resistant. An umbel has up to 30 blossoms. It starts blooming late, but continues through the summer until fall.

SPECIAL QUALITIES: A classic among Ground Covers and very popular as a decorative tree too. This robust variety is frost-resistant and tolerates hot, sunny locations as well as half-shade. Its leaves will catch your eye with their yellow color in fall.

USAGE: "The Fairy" is suitable as an individual, a Bed Rose or in groups of 4 – 5 plants per square yard/meter as a Ground Cover for plains and hillsides. You can combine it well with perennials and heather gardens. It is recommended for graves and looks good hanging from walls. With its overhanging branches, it is perfect for hanging pots or as a potted tree. The flowers last a long time in a vase.

VARIETIES: "Fairy Queen" shines with its crimson-red, full flowers and is similar to the mother plant. The same holds true for "Heidekind," with its cherry-red flower clusters.

PLANTING GROUND COVERS IN PLANTERS

With their overhanging branches, many Ground Covers are very well-suited for planters and patio pots. True-rooted varieties also do well with little space for roots. Heat-resistant varieties can also border rock gardens. Remember, however, that the pot should be covered with a kind of foil or insulation material in winter.

CLIMBING ARTISTS AMONG ROSES

Few rose varieties need so little room and offer such beautiful flowers as Climbing Roses. They can change cold walls into blooming rose curtains or make arcades and arbors green and romantic. Two or three roses in a pyramid or on a column certainly catch your eye. And can you imagine a nicer entrance to your garden than a gate decorated with roses?

Even the smallest garden has a place for climbing roses. These varieties – which do well in large pots – also grow well on balconies. The rose must be attached to a solid structure. Climbing Roses are basically Shrub Roses with long shoots, but they lack fixing parts – such as bines or anchor roots. Climbing structures of wood or steel are especially stable. They should be situated at least 3 – 4 in (8 – 10 cm) away from the wall so that air can circulate freely.

Climbing Roses bloom in many different styles one or more times a season. Ramblers grow quickly – they are mostly once-blooming Climbing Roses with very long, thin shoots. They like to twist around trees and grow rapidly towards the light at the same time. Each variety, old or new, has its own special charm.

"Adélaide d'Orléans" Rose

ORIGIN: Cultivation, Jacques 1826.

APPEARANCE: A rambler with long, thin shoots, quickly grows to 15 ft (4.5 m) tall and 10 ft (3 m) wide.

FLOWERS: The flower clusters consist of many small, half-full flowers, whose tender pink turns creamy. They hang in cascades from shoots, concealing the leaves nearly completely and spreading a pleasant fragrance reminiscent of peonies. After the main blooming period in summer, several others follow.

SPECIAL QUALITIES: "Adélaide d'Orléans" is an offspring of *rosa sempervirens* and is one of the oldest Climbing Roses. It was cultivated in France. The flowers of this rose group always grow in dense clusters, the shoots have almost no thorns and the dense leaves usually last through the winter.

USAGE: This well-growing, robust rambler quickly makes walls and climbing structures of all kinds green. It likes to climb on trees. At the same time, it tolerates soil lacking humus as well as half-shade.

SMALL VARIETIES: "Félicité et Perpétue" is also an old *rosa sempervirens*. It is characterized by pompom-like, fragrant flowers in creamy white and is similar to "Adélaide d'Orléans." Trees of this variety are very decorative.

HOW TO BECOME AN EXPERT ON CLIMBERS

If they do not have enough space, pruning ramblers is recommended so that the plant does not look untidy. This means you simply cut off some old, heavily branched shoots near the ground in early spring. It is recommended to do such rejuvenation only exceptionally with more shrubby-growing varieties.

"Alchymist" Rose

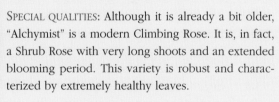

Location:
☼ – ☼

Qualities:
❀ ⌐

ORIGIN: Cultivation, Kordes 1956.

APPEARANCE: Bushy, upright, medium-fast growth, 11 ½ ft (3.5 m) tall and 8 ft (2.5 m) wide. The shoots have many thorns.

FLOWERS: The dense, full flowers are yellow-orange and reddish when fading. They have an old-fashioned shape and are mostly open quartered. They appear in early summer and late blooming flowers often have stronger colors than the early ones. Their fragrance resembles a mixture of tea and honey and the flowers contrast wonderfully with the bright green to bronze leaves.

SPECIAL QUALITIES: Although it is already a bit older, "Alchymist" is a modern Climbing Rose. It is, in fact, a Shrub Rose with very long shoots and an extended blooming period. This variety is robust and characterized by extremely healthy leaves.

USAGE: For growing on walls, patios, fences or other structures. This variety is also suitable as a Shrub Rose and grows satisfactorily in soil lacking nutrients and in half-shade.

"American Pillar" Rose

ORIGIN: cultivation, van Fleet 1902.

APPEARANCE: rambler, quickly growing, 13 – 20 ft (4 – 6 m) tall and up to 10 ft (3 m) wide.

FLOWERS: The simple, crimson flowers look very lively with their white eyes. They open cup-shaped, revealing yellow anthers. The giant flower clusters contrast with the glossy, green leaves. The blooming period lasts from June to July.

SPECIAL QUALITIES: An old, amply blooming offspring of the quick growing *rosa wichuraiana* which has lost nothing of its charm to this day. Because it is a bit susceptible to powdery mildew, you need to choose an optimal location for it.

USAGE: Like all ramblers, this variety is suitable for impatient gardeners who want to quickly adorn bare walls and unsightly places in their gardens. They also give trellises and arcades a charming look and they like to climb on trees. This rose is frost-resistant and tolerates sanday, nutrient-deficient soil and half-shade.

Location:
☼ – ☼

Qualities:
❀ ↄ

"Blaze Superior" Rose

Location:
☼ – ☀

Qualities:
✿✿ ♪

Usage:
✂

ORIGIN: Cultivation, Jackson and Perkins 1954. Also known as "Demokracie."

APPEARANCE: Rambler, quick growing, branches slightly hanging, 10 – 13 ft (3 – 4 m) tall and wide.

FLOWERS: The fiery, scarlet-red flowers, reminiscent of the Tea Hybrid, charm everybody. They appear in clusters all summer above dark-green leaves. Moreover, they have a beautiful fragrance. This rose blooms after the main blooming period until fall.

SPECIAL QUALITIES: The robust character of this multiple-blooming climber is combined with the stunning beauty of its flowers. It is a superior variation of the well-known "Blaze," which also charms you with its big, full, scarlet flowers.

USAGE: This quickly growing climber is also suitable for less sunny locations and even tolerates sandy soil lacking nutrients. It grows quickly on trees and greens walls, pergolas and similar structures, but it needs a lot of space. Its intensely bright flowers look very festive in a vase.

"Compassion" Rose

ORIGIN: cultivation, Harkness 1974.

APPEARANCE: a broad bush, medium-quick growth, 5 – 8 ft (1.5 – 2.5 m) tall, in warm regions without heavy frost even taller, up to 6 ft (1.8 m) wide.

FLOWERS: The big, full flowers show a sportive play of color. They are light pink with a touch of apricot in efflorescence, silver-pink later and faded when wilting. They are similar to Tea Hybrids in shape and at the same time they are very big, with diameters of 4 – 5 in (10 – 12 cm). They usually grow individually on long stems and only seldom in small clusters. They have a sweet fragrance and continue to bloom until fall.

SPECIAL QUALITIES: This multiple-blooming climber is characterized by an intense fragrance. It is a bit sensitive to frost and it is recommended for regions with a mild climate. It was praised by ADR in 1976.

USAGE: Because it doest not grow too big, this rose is a good choice for pyramids and columns. It can also grow freely as a shrub. Its long stems make it ideal for cutting. Prune the parts damaged by frost as you do Bed Roses.

Location:
☼

Qualities:
✿✿ ↷

Usage:
✄

"Dortmund" Rose

ORIGIN: Cultivation, Kordes 1955.

APPEARANCE: Upright, hanging bent branches, 7 – 13 ft (2 – 4 m) tall and up to 6 ft (1.8 m) wide according to its location.

FLOWERS: The simple, cup-shaped flowers are deep red and look at us with white eyes. The petals are slightly wavy and the individual flowers are up to 4 in (10 cm) wide. They form big clusters that nearly hide the glossy, dark-green, wavy leaves. They bloom several times after the main blooming period in summer. The rose spreads a pleasant fragrance.

FRUIT: Many hips.

SPECIAL QUALITIES: A robust climbing shrub, not demanding as to location. It grows in full sun as well as in half-shade, and is frost and rain-resistant. It was awarded an ADR predicate in 1954.

USAGE: This rambler looks nice individually or in groups. It grows almost everywhere and brightens walls, lanes and pergolas of all types nicely.

SIMILAR VARIETIES: "Maria Lisa" blooms crimson-pink with a white center and reveals eye-catching yellow anthers. "Hiawatha" is an old, quick growing variety which charms you with its simple flowers ranging from purple to violet.

A PLACE IN THE SUN

Although roses love sun, a southern wall is not an ideal location for them since walls reflect sunshine and accumulate warmth, rendering the roses very warm and dry. Spider mites and powdery mildew fungus thrive in such conditions. Walls facing south-east or southwest are most suitable, if there is adequate air circulation.

"Flammentanz" Rose

ORIGIN: Cultivation, Kordes 1955.

APPEARANCE: Rambler, upright, overhanging branches, quick growing, 10 – 16 ft (3 – 5 m) tall.

FLOWERS: The dense, full flowers catch the eye from afar with their shiny blood-red petals. They grow in big clusters and keep their bright color even when fading. The vivid red harmonizes with the dark-green leaves touched by a copper glow. Flowers are bounteous, but there is no second bloom.

SPECIAL QUALITIES: This quick growing climbing giant combines robustness with shiny red, beautiful flowers, which explains why it was praised by the ADR in 1952.

USAGE: This frost-resistant variety enjoys every location. It tolerates full sun as well as half-shade and it can stand individually or in groups. It also grows lying on the ground without a climbing structures and quickly greens large areas. The fiery red "Flammentanz" can be enjoyed as a tree or as a potted plant. It is suitable for planting on columns and on pyramids.

SMALL VARIETIES: "Paul's Scarlet Climber" has many good qualities as a legacy for "Flammentanz." The variety emerged as early as in 1916. It charms you with its deep-red, dense, round flowers. This rose is a bit smaller, growing to 7 – 8 ft (2 – 2.5 m) and has a sweet fragrance.

SUPPORT BLOOMING

Climbers tend to grow quickly towards the sun, sprouting just a few side shoots and flowers. Concentrate on the tops of the shoots. If you tie the shoots as horizontally as possible while rising, they sprout many side shoots and thus more flowers.

"Gerbe Rose" Rose

ORIGIN: Cultivation, Fauque 1904.

APPEARANCE: Quickly growing, up to 20 ft (6 m) tall and 15 ft (4.5 m) wide.

FLOWERS: The dense, full flowers are a pretty pink. The flower center is darker and more yellowish. The flowers grow in small clusters that bloom abundantly in summer and are accompanied by a fruity, apple-like fragrance. This rose does not bloom repeatedly.

SPECIAL QUALITIES: This offspring of the quickly growing *rosa wichuraiana*, ancestor of many climbers, is a curiosity among old climbers.

USAGE: A quickly growing rambler that tolerates sun and half-shade. It is especially suitable for impatient gardeners who want to hide walls and less attractive spots in their gardens in a short time. It also grows well near water.

SIMILAR VARIETIES: "Albertine" – with strongly fragrant, pink flowers – also grows very tall.

Location:
☀ – ☀

Qualities:
❀ ♪

"Gloire de Dijon" Rose

ORIGIN: Cultivation, Jacotot 1853. This French variety was also known as "Old Glory Rose" in old English cottage gardens.

APPEARANCE: Upright, quick growing, 10 – 13 ft (3 – 4 m) tall, up to 8 ft (2.5 m) wide.

FLOWERS: The big, strongly fragrant flowers feature many color tones ranging from pale yellow and apricot to orange. They are densely packed and open quartered. A second bloom often appears in fall after the main blooming period in summer.

SPECIAL QUALITIES: This very old climbing rose has the Bourbon Rose "Souvenir de la Malmaison" as a parent. It prefers mild regions with few showers and the leaves are slightly susceptible to black spots. This curiosity enriches every rose garden in spite of this disadvantage.

USAGE: This especially nice variety is recommended for warm, protected house walls. It catches the eye when trained out like a fan.

Location:

Qualities:

"Goldener Olymp" Rose

ORIGIN: Cultivation, Kordes 1984.

APPEARANCE: Upright, shrubby to climbing, medium-strong, 5 – 6 ft (1.5 – 1.8 m) tall.

FLOWERS: The golden-yellow flowers have a touch of copper and turn yellow towards the rims. They are loosely packed and have wavy petals. They are very big, with diameters of 4 in (10 cm). They form luxurious umbels which contrast nicely with the dark-green leaves. Moreover, they have a tender fragrance.

SPECIAL QUALITIES: This variety is especially recommended for mild regions or sheltered locations. Its shiny flowers are clearly visible from a distance.

USAGE: This climber for every occasion can also be grown as a shrub rose. It is suitable for walls and climbing structures of all types.

SIMILAR VARIETIES: "Goldstern" has golden-yellow, bright, full flowers and grows as a Shrub or a Climbing Rose. "Golden Showers" blooms lemon-yellow and grows up to 10 ft (3 m) tall. The golden-yellow "Goldfassade" has a rich fragrance.

THE RIGHT PLANS ARE CRUCIAL

First, determine how big the climbing structure should be because once the rose has spread, it is very difficult to enlarge the space it covers. Harmonize the floral color of your roses with the colors and structures of the wall it grows on. For example, red flowers are not visible enough on red bricks, light walls are not suitable backgrounds for white or cream-colored flowers. Guide your rose – when young, if possible – in the desired direction. Shoots can be bent without problems. Once it has grown, it is not possible to change the rose's shape. Do not bind shoots too firmly to the structure because you risk strangling them as they grow bigger.

"Harlekin" Rose

ORIGIN: Cultivation, Kordes 1986.

APPEARANCE: Upright, shrubby, well-branched, hanging shoots, 7 – 10 ft (2 – 3 m) tall.

FLOWERS: The dense, full, rosette-shaped flowers are creamy white, and the wide, red rims give them a certain charm. They are very big, with diameters of 4 – 5 (10 -12 cm), and have a strong fragrance. This variety blooms repeatedly, with a long main blooming period.

SPECIAL QUALITIES: A multi-aspect climber with old-fashioned charm.

USAGE: This cheerfully colored variety is suitable for greening arcades, arbors and walls and also tolerates southern exposures. You can plant it individually or in groups. The rose may also be potted, and its sporty flowers make bouquets very festive.

> **DIRECTION CHANGE**
> Climbers do not grow exclusively towards the sun. They can also look very nice when growing down from the top of a wall.

"Kir Royal" Rose

ORIGIN: cultivation, Meilland 1995.

APPEARANCE: upright, bushy shrub, overhanging branches, 7 – 10 ft (2 – 3 m) tall.

FLOWERS: Light-pink, full flowers develop from reddish round buds. The irregular spots of red catch your eye. The cup-shaped flowers gather in loose clusters with wavy petals. The light color of the flowers harmonizes very nicely with the light-green leaves. The slightly fragrant flowers are medium-sized, with diameters of 3 in (7 cm). The main blooming period is in mid-summer and after that this rose blooms only sporadically.

SPECIAL QUALITIES: A modern, hardy variety with an old-fashioned flower shape. This plant can withstand frost and its leaves are resistant to powdery mildew and black spots.

USAGE: If you are a romantic, this rose is an ideal choice for beautifying climbing structures and walls of all types. It can be planted individually or in groups.

Location:
 ☀

Qualities:

"Leverkusen" Rose

Location:
☼ – ☀

Qualities:
❀❀❀ 👃

Usage:
🪴 🌳

ORIGIN: Cultivation, Kordes 1954.

APPEARANCE: Upright, quick growing, up to 10 ft (3 m) tall and 8.2 (2.5 m) wide.

FLOWERS: The lemon-yellow flowers are half-full and open like cups. The wavy petals give this rose a special charm and it releases a tender, sweet fragrance. The dark-green, glossy leaves set off the tender yellow flower clusters very well. Their blooming period is almost continuous.

SPECIAL QUALITIES: "Leverkusen" is a robust, continuous bloomer with healthy, strong leaves. Because it is highly frost-resistant, it is even recommended for the coldest locations.

USAGE: This climber is suitable for all situations and also grows well in sandy, nutrient-deficient soil and half-shade. It looks good in rose-arches or on columns, or as a potted tree.

SIMILAR VARIETIES: The quick growing variety "Parkdirektor Riggers" – with velvety, blood-red flowers – originates from the same robust mother plant.

"Lykkefund" Rose

ORIGIN: Cultivation, Olsen 1930.

APPEARANCE: Upright, very quick growing, up to 23 ft (7 m) tall and 15 ft (4.5 m) wide; shoots have almost no thorns.

FLOWERS: The simple flowers are creamy yellow with a touch of pink. They turn nearly white while fading. They grow in big clusters and spread an intense fragrance. Their pretty color contrasts with the light-green, bronze leaves especially well. This rose blooms richly, but only once.

SPECIAL QUALITIES: This old variety is a curiosity among climbers and its popularity is increasing. It is a successful hybrid of the thornless "Zéphirine Drouhin" and the quickly growing *rosa helenae*.

USAGE: "Lykkefund" grows quickly on walls and large climbing structures and climbs on trees especially well. It also tolerates soil lacking humus and half-shade. That is why it is especially suitable to cheer up dark areas in your garden.

Location:
☼ – ☼

Qualities:
❀ ↵

"Morning Jewel" Rose

Location:

Qualities:

Usage:

ORIGIN: Cultivation, Cocker 1968.

APPEARANCE: Bushy shrub, upright, partly hanging branches, quick growing, 7 – 10 ft (2 -3 m) tall, up to 8 ft (2.5 m) wide.

FLOWERS: The crimson-red flowers, possessing an intense fragrance, are loosely packed, cup-shaped and reach diameters of 4 – 5 in (10 - 12 cm). They usually grow individually or sometimes in groups of two. This variety blooms richly and more than just once in a season.

SPECIAL QUALITIES: This robust variety with a beautiful fragrance is an offspring of the well-known "New Dawn" Climbing Rose. It was awarded an ADR predicate in 1975.

USAGE: Adds charm to arbors, arcades, rose-arches or other climbing structures. It is available as a decorative tree as well.

CLIMBING ROSES IN POTS

Rose trees or cascades are Climbing Roses cultivated as trees.

"New Dawn" Rose

ORIGIN: Cultivation, Sommerset 1930.

APPEARANCE: Upright, bushy shrub, hanging branches, quick growing, 10 – 13 ft (3 – 4 m) tall and up to 8 ft (2.5 m) wide.

FLOWERS: The half-full, cup-shaped flowers charm you with their mild pearl-pink color and equally lovely fragrance. They are medium-sized, with a diameter of 2 – 3 in (6 – 8 cm). This variety also blooms after the main blooming period in summer.

FRUIT: This rose yields many hips.

SPECIAL QUALITIES: This robust climbing giant grows in nearly any location, in direct sunshine or in half-shade. Furthermore, it is very frost-resistant and can withstand harsh locations.

USAGE: This multi-functional rose greens climbing structures of all types, grows decoratively down walls and enjoys large pots. The light flowers contrast beautifully with dark backgrounds. This rose is available as a decorative tree as well, and its flowers last a long time in a vase.

Location:
☼ – ☼

Qualities:
✿✿ ↷ ✿

Usage:
🪣 🪴 ✂

"Paul Noël" Rose

Location:

☼ – ☀

Qualities:
❀ ⌣

Usage:
🪴 🌶

ORIGIN: Cultivation, Tanne 1913.

APPEARANCE: Upright, quickly growing, 10 – 16 ft (3 - 5 m) tall and 5 – 6½ ft (1.5 – 2 m) wide. It creeps along the ground with long, thin shoots when deprived of a climbing structure.

FLOWERS: The salmon-pink flowers are densely packed and rosette-shaped. They are relatively small, with diameters of 1 – 2 in (3 – 4 cm), but they give off an intense fragrance. Although this variety is once-blooming, a second or even third bloom may be expected.

SPECIAL QUALITIES: This quick-growing rambler is an ideal choice for impatient gardeners who like an old-fashioned flower shape and an intense fragrance.

USAGE: This variety is a good choice for growing on arcades, arbors and lanes. An especially elegant look is created if you let it grow down a wall. It quickly greens up large surfaces when creeping on the ground. You can make a patio very romantic with a potted tree of this variety.

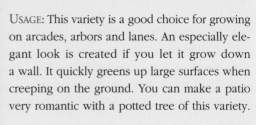

"*Raubritter*" *Rose*

ORIGIN: Cultivation, Kordes 1936.

APPEARANCE: Upright, bushy shrub, densely branched, 7 – 10 ft (2 – 3 m) tall. The long, thin shoots have many thorns.

FLOWERS: The dense, ball-shaped flowers are a light magenta and possess cup-shaped blossoms of up to 2 in (5 cm) wide. They bloom either individually or in big umbels, spreading a light fragrance. Their color contrasts nicely with the dark-green leaves.

SPECIAL QUALITIES: If you like luxurious flower balls with antique charm, this variety is the right choice for you. This rose also enjoys half-shade, but an airy location is necessary because, without sufficient ventilation, the rose is susceptible to powdery mildew.

USAGE: "Raubritter" is a multi-functional variety that may be used as a Climbing or a Shrub Rose with equal success. It looks especially good when hanging down a wall. It quickly makes large areas green when grown on the ground and it is excellent for stabilizing hillsides. This rose is also an eye-catcher as a tree.

Location:
☼ – ☼

Qualities:
✿ ↷

Usage:
🏺 🌱

"Rosarium Uetersen" Rose

ORIGIN: Cultivation, Kordes 1977.

APPEARANCE: Upright, ample, hanging branches, slow to medium-quick growing climber up to 9 ft (3 m) tall. As a shrub, up to 6 ft (2 m) and about 6 ft (1.8 m) wide.

FLOWERS: The bright pink flowers are rosette-shaped and luxuriously packed with up to 100 petals. They grow up to 3 in (8 cm) across and turn silver-pink when fading. They appear early in summer and bloom either individually or usually, 10 – 20 blossoms to a cluster at the tops of long shoots. They have a tender Wild-Rose-like fragrance. They also bloom after the main blooming period.

SPECIAL QUALITIES: With its large flower balls, "Rosarium Uetersen" makes any place look romantic. It is multi-functional and tolerates nearly all locations, even hot, sunny ones and half-shade. It is not easily damaged by frost and longer showers.

USAGE: This rose beautifies walls when climbing on structures. It is suitable for pyramids and columns as well. Because the variety does not grow as big as many other climbers, it can also be grown as a shrub. Cascade roses

are suitable as potted plants and can enhance a balcony
garden beautifully.

A Strong Team: Roses and Clematis

They look perfect together and produce an elegant flower combination.
Pay attention to the similar strength of both so that the combination
works well. It is best to combine multiple-blooming roses with Clematis
varieties that bloom in summer. Roots should not be exposed to sunshine.
Plant roses and clematis together in pots as well.

"Rote Flamme" Rose

Location:

☼

Qualities:

❀❀

ORIGIN: Cultivation, Kordes 1967.

APPEARANCE: Upright, bushy shrub, many branches, quick growing, up to 4 m tall.

FLOWERS: The dense, full flowers with a classic, round shape shine a deep red. They are very big, with diameters of 4 – 5 in (10 – 12 cm). The flower clusters grow on the top of the shoots and contrast with the dark-green, glossy leaves. The first blooming period is luxurious in summer while further blooming periods are a bit weaker.

SPECIAL QUALITIES: If you want to get visible results quickly and like loud colors, you should choose "Rote Flamme."

USAGE: This quickly growing variety quickly greens walls, arbors and climbing structures of any type.

SIMILAR VARIETIES: "Gruß an Heidelberg" and "Sympathie," by the same cultivator, are recommended for lovers of dark-red tones. "Santana," by Tantau and "Colonia" by Meilland, have a similar tender fragrance.

"Super Dorothy" Rose

ORIGIN: Cultivation, Hetzel 1986.

APPEARANCE: Rambler, climbs on any structure or lies on the ground without support; long, bent shoots, 10 – 16 ft (3 – 5 m) tall or long.

FLOWERS: The small, pink flowers open cup-shaped and are luxuriously packed with petals. The individual blossoms are only 1 in (3 cm) wide, but 20 of them grow in an umbel. This variety blooms until fall after the main blooming period in summer.

SPECIAL QUALITIES: "Super Dorothy" reflects its name. It grows quickly and blooms – very unusually for a rambler – richly and continuously. The small leaves show that it also tolerates hot locations.

USAGE: It quickly makes walls nice and beautifies arbors, arcades, etc. If you let it grow on the ground, it covers bare areas very quickly. 1 plant per square yard/meter is enough. Trees trained from it are very nice and are suitable as potted plants, too.

SIMILAR VARIETIES: "Super Excelsa" blooms crimson.

Location:
☼ – ☼

Qualities:
❀❀❀

Usage:
🪣 🌱

"Veilchenblau" Rose

Location:
☼ – ☼

Qualities:
❀ 〰

ORIGIN: Cultivation, Schmidt 1909. An offspring of *rosa multiflora*

APPEARANCE: Upright, dense bush, quick growing, 10– 13 ft (3 – 4 m) tall. The shoots have nearly no thorns

FLOWERS: The cup-shaped, half-full flowers are purple with white eyes. They seem nearly blue sometimes and possibly white-striped while wilting. They are small and have many blossoms which grow in dense umbels. They are accompanied by a tender, orange fragrance and have narrow, matte-green, feathery leaves. The blooming period covers June and July and there is no second bloom.

SPECIAL QUALITIES: A rose for lovers of unusual colors. Also tolerates half-shade.

USAGE: "Veilchenblau," grows happily on walls and lanes. It has everything you can ask of a climber. But the color of the flowers cannot be combined with any color. White is best here.

SIMILAR VARIETIES: It is difficult to imitate the color of "Veilchenblau," but there are several varieties similar to it.

"Rose Marie Vieaud" is one of them, a spontaneous off-spring of this 1924 variety. Its flowers are more densely packed and redder and the plant grows up to 16 ft (5 m) tall. "Bleu Magenta," without thorns, blooms purple and changes later to a violet-blue.

FINE ROSES WITHOUT THORNS
"Zéphirine Drouhin," a climber, is the first rose without thorns. It was cultivated as early as 1868 in France. Its thornless, loosely packed and pleasantly scented bright pink to light red flowers make it an attractive choice.

"Venusta Pendula" Rose

Location:

Qualities:

ORIGIN: The old variety is an Ayrshire Rose, which originated from the climber or Field Rose *rosa arvensis*, native to Europe. It inherited its creeping or climbing shoots from its ancestors. The precise origin is not known. It was introduced in Germany by W. Kordes in 1928.

APPEARANCE: Rambler, loosely packed, quick growing, long hanging shoots, creeps on the ground or on a climbing structure up to 16 ft (5 m) tall and 5 ft (1.5 m) wide.

FLOWERS: The cup-shaped, open, loosely packed flowers are white with pretty pink rims. The individual flowers are medium-sized, with diameters of 2 – 3 in (5 – 7 cm). The matte-green leaves create a contrasting background. This variety blooms only once in June or July, but abundantly.

SPECIAL QUALITIES: This vital, frost-resistant and easily grown rambler deserves your selection. Because it tolerates half-shade, it is especially suitable for dark garden corners or walls that need cheering up without much effort by the gardener.

USAGE: This rose quickly changes arcades and arbors into rose rooms. It likes to climb on walls and trees. Its antique charm is ideal for rose arcades. If you do not bind it to a climbing structure, it grows on the ground and changes bare places into blooming rose carpets.

SIMILAR VARIETIES: "Bobbie James" is a very popular rambler with white, half-full flowers and a strong fragrance. "Sanders' White Rambler" is not tall at 12 ft (3.5 m), but it does grow very bushy with strong branches. The white, rosette-shaped flowers appear in big, hanging clusters in summer and have a sweet fragrance.

The Luxurious Floral Beauty of Shrub Roses

Shrub Roses beautify our gardens as decorative trees. While the modern varieties bloom either continuously or in two blooming periods, mid-season and late-season, the ample floral beauty of Wild and Park Roses blooms just once, but for weeks on end. Park Roses are the cultivated offspring of Wild Roses. The latter are very robust, frost-resistant and strong. Shrub Roses focus much energy in flowers and thus remain small. Many of them grow "only" 3 – 5 ft (1 – 1.5 m) tall, others 6 ft (2 m) or taller. Upright growing varieties are best suited for small gardens and blooming hedges, while wild growing plants with over-hanging branches need more space. The flower shape ranges from simple and primitive blooms to elegant, Tea-Rose-like shapes. Simple flowers are especially beloved as a source of nectar for bees, bumble-bees, butterflies and others. Shrub Roses are an eye-catching individual plant because of their striking shape. They should be planted in prominent places because they are among the most vibrantly blooming roses. If you have enough space, you can make groups of two to three plants and create enormous shrubs. Shrub Roses, which include many Old and English Roses, combine well with other decorative trees.

"Angela" Rose

Location:

Qualities:

Usage:

ORIGIN: Cultivation, Kordes 1984.

APPEARANCE: Shrubby, upright, loosely packed, medium-quickly growing, 3 – 5 ft (1 – 1.5 m) tall.

FLOWERS: The pink, half-full flowers have an old-time charm. They are lighter in the center and show their yellow anthers clearly. The open, cup-shaped flowers are medium-sized, with a diameter of 2 – 3 in (4 – 6 cm). They appear in big clusters nearly continuously until fall and have a light fragrance.

SPECIAL QUALITIES: This robust rose can withstand errors in care. It enjoys sun as well as half-shade and its flowers tolerate longer showers too. It was awarded an ADR premium in 1982.

USAGE: This compact plant is ideal for small gardens where you can plant it individually or in groups. Up to 3 plants are planted per square yard/meter according to how dense you want the plants to be. It is suitable for hedges and goes well with perennials. The rose looks good potted on a balcony.

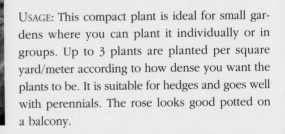

"Bischofsstadt Paderborn" Rose

ORIGIN: Cultivation, Kordes 1964.

Appearance: Shrubby, upright, richly branched, 3 – 5 ft (1 – 1.5 m) tall, up to 3 ft (1 m) wide.

Location:
☼ – ☼

Qualities:
✿✿

FLOWERS: The orange to cinnamon-red flowers, with a velvet gloss, develop from crimson-red, drop-shaped buds. They are simple to half-full, cup-shaped and about 3 in (8 cm) across. The floral center is yellowish white. They grow in loose, narrow clusters above green, slightly glossy, initially reddish leaves and bloom until early fall.

SPECIAL QUALITIES: This classic with shiny red flowers was awarded an ADR predicate in 1968.

USAGE: The red flowers catch your eye from a distance whether the plants grow individually or in groups. Because this variety also grows in half-shade, it brings color to dark garden plots. You can let it grow in a hedge without pruning. 1 – 2 plants are recommended per square yard/meter. Keep the distance between individual plants at about 32 in (80 cm) in hedges. This rose is also valuable as a source of pollen.

"Colette" Rose

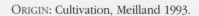

Location:
☀

Qualities:
✿✿✿ ⌇

Usage:
🪣 ✂ ✗

ORIGIN: Cultivation, Meilland 1993.

APPEARANCE: Upright, bushy, strongly branched, up to 6 ft (2 m) tall and 3 ft (1 m) wide.

FLOWERS: The densely packed, rosette-shaped flowers resemble Old Roses. They are salmon-pink and when they wilt, a golden-brown hue can be seen in the middle. They are quite large, with diameters of 3 in (8 cm). The floral clusters harmonize well with the medium-green leaves.

SPECIAL QUALITIES: This amply blooming variety spreads an antiquated charm with its luxurious flower balls and pleasant fragrance. It is not susceptible to powdery mildew or black spots.

USAGE: This impressive Shrub Rose may be planted individually or in groups of 2 in a space of 6 square ft (2 square meters).

SIMILAR VARIETIES: The light-pink "Eden Rose 85," the "Romantic Roses" cultivated by the French cultivator Meilland, is also characterized by dense flower balls.

"Darthuizer Orange Fire" Rose

ORIGIN: Cultivation, Ilsink/Pekmez 1987.

APPEARANCE: Wide bush, thickly branched, up to 5 ft (1.5 m) tall.

FLOWERS: The flowers are shiny orange to light red, but the buds are dark red. They open cup-shaped and grow in loose clusters above slightly glossy leaves. The wavy petals are especially charming. This variety blooms repeatedly.

SPECIAL QUALITIES: An eye-catching color to top off every garden.

USAGE: This rose may be planted individually in groups or in hedges. It is recommended that about 32 in (80 cm) between plants be maintained in a hedge and 1 plant is enough for 1 square yard/meter.

SIMILAR VARIETIES: "Brilliant" has fiery orange, full flowers with a tender Wild-Rose-like fragrance. The full flowers of "Feuerwerk" are the same shiny orange. Both varieties grow up to 5 ft (1.5 m) tall.

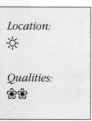

Location:
☼

Qualities:
❀❀

"Dirigent" Rose

ORIGIN: Cultivation, Tantau 1956.

APPEARANCE: Upright, wide shrub, moderately quick-growing, 5 – 6 ft (1.5 – 1.8 m) tall, 3 – 5 ft (1 – 1.2 m) wide.

FLOWERS: The blood-red flowers are half-full and open cup-shaped. They are quite large, with diameters of 3 in (8 cm). Because many of them grow in a cluster, they are quite dramatic. The blooms contrast nicely with their glossy, green leaves.

SPECIAL QUALITIES: This robust variety combines its unique, shiny color with a non-stop, rich bloom. It was praised by ADR as early as in 1958 and it is just as popular now as it was then.

USAGE: This Shrub Rose looks lovely individually or in groups. It needs enough space to develop its nice shape. It is well-suited for hedges, where it grows without pruning. The distance between plants should be 5 – 6½ ft (1.5 – 2 m) if planted individually, 28 – 32 in (70 – 80 cm) in hedges. It tolerates hot, sunny locations as well as longer showers. It is a popular pollen source for insects.

"Dornröschen" Rose

ORIGIN: Cultivation, Kordes 1960. A hybrid of *rosa acicularis*.

APPEARANCE: Upright, bushy, medium-quickly growing, 3 – 5 ft (1 – 1.5 m) tall and wide.

FLOWERS: The full, Tea-Rose-shaped flowers are vivid, dark pink. Up to 10 of them grow in an umbel and each blossom is 2 – 3 in (6 – 8 cm) in diameter. The blooming period covers the months of June and July.

FRUIT: Hips grow especially thickly on unpruned plants in fall.

SPECIAL QUALITIES: "Dornröschen" is a once-blooming Shrub Rose, but it sometimes blooms weakly again in the fall. It blooms amply and early.

USAGE: This rose, with its noble flowers, is an attractive individual shrub. It is suitable for small gardens. If you have more space, plant it in groups. It grows in hedges without pruning. The distance between individual plants should be 5 – 6 ft (1.5 – 2 m), or 3 – 5 ft (1 – 1.5 m) in groups.

Location:
☼

Qualities:
❀ ⚘

"Erfurt" Rose

Location:

☼ – ☼

Qualities:

🌸🌸 👃

ORIGIN: Cultivation, Kordes 1939.

APPEARANCE: Upright, slightly hanging branches, quick growing, up to 5 ft (1.5 m) tall and 4 ft (1.2 m) wide.

FLOWERS: The cup-shaped, simple flowers are pink with white-yellow centers and eye-catching brown anthers. They appear continuously throughout the season and are accompanied by a light fragrance. The floral color contrasts nicely with the dark-green, slightly glossy leaves.

SPECIAL QUALITIES: Although it has been on the market for a long time, this sporty, robust variety with Wild-Rose-charm has lost none of its popularity.

USAGE: This Shrub Rose is suitable individually or in groups. It is a good choice for hedges and tolerates half-shade as well as nutrient-deficient soil.

SIMILAR VARIETIES: "Angelina," cultivated by the Englishman Cocker, originated in the year 1976. It has very loosely packed, pink flowers with light centers and an intense fragrance. Because it stays a bit small, it is ideal for potting.

"Felicitas" Rose

ORIGIN: Cultivation, Kordes 1998.

APPEARANCE: Wide shrub, bushy, hanging shoots, up to 32 in (80 cm) tall and 5 ft (1.5 m) wide.

FLOWERS: The simple, medium-sized flowers are a bright crimson. The yellow anthers contrast nicely with the red blooms. The individual blossoms grow in umbels above green, very glossy leaves, and have an intense fragrance.

SPECIAL QUALITIES: This variety is truly multi-functional and robust. It was awarded an ADR predicate in 1998.

USAGE: This rose is a good ground-covering solitaire, if you have enough room. Groups offer you even more beautiful flowers. Because it has long branches, it can cover large areas quickly.

SIMILAR VARIETIES: "Northern Lights" charm you with dark-pink flowers, which may be simple or slightly packed. It is suitable as a Ground Cover as well.

Location:
☼

Qualities:

"Ferdy" Rose

Location:

Qualities:

Usage:

ORIGIN: Cultivation, Suzuki/Keisei Nursery 1984.

APPEARANCE: Bushy shrub, densely branched, overhanging shoots and many thorns, 24 – 35 in (60 – 90 cm) tall and nearly as wide.

FLOWERS: The full flowers are bright salmon-pink with yellow centers. They are cup-shaped and quite small, with diameters of 2 in (4 cm). The dense clusters of flowers line the branches like strings of pearls and nearly hide the glossy green, feathery leaves.

SPECIAL QUALITIES: This beloved Japanese hybrid charms you with its dense flowers and hardiness. It is absolutely resistant to powdery mildew and black spots. It should not be pruned regularly because it blooms on two years' shoots. Only prune it if absolutely necessary.

USAGE: A multi-functional variety that may be used either decoratively by itself or as a Ground Cover. It goes well with loose hedges too. You can let it grow down a wall with its hanging branches. It is very frost-resistant and enjoys a pot.

"Freisinger Morgenröte" Rose

ORIGIN: Cultivation, Kordes 1988.

APPEARANCE: bushy shrub, quickly growing, 4 – 5 ft (1.2 – 1.5 m) tall.

FLOWERS: The round, densely-packed flowers resemble Noble Roses. They are yellow with a touch of orange and are pinkish red towards the rims. They are very big, with diameters of 5 in (12 cm) and outward-rolling petals give them a special charm. Furthermore, they have a strong fragrance. The dense clusters grow above bright green, glossy leaves.

SPECIAL QUALITIES: This robust rose is the right choice for lovers of happy hues and romantic floral shapes.

USAGE: A nicely shaped Shrub Rose, it is ideal individually. The color effect is even stronger if it is planted in groups or in hedges. The tender color play of the flowers contrasts nicely with the dark background.

SIMILAR VARIETIES: The full, amber-yellow flowers of "Caramella" have romantic, wavy petals.

Location:
☼

Qualities:
✿✿ ⌒

Usage:
✂ ✗

"Frühlingsduft" Rose

ORIGIN: Cultivation, Kordes 1949. A hybrid of *rosa spinosissima* "Altaica" (see pimpinellifolia above).

APPEARANCE: Upright, shrubby, overhanging branches, up to 6 ft (3 m) tall and 6½ ft (1.8 – 2 m) wide.

FLOWERS: The big, dense, full flowers are lemon-yellow at first and then turn pink. They appear in spring and spread an intense fragrance. They contrast nicely with their dark-green, wavy petals.

SPECIAL QUALITIES: As a hybrid of *rosa spinosissima*, this variety has lost neither its robustness nor its antique charm. Always a beloved rose in country gardens, it delights you with the first roses of the year.

USAGE: This big, undemanding shrub enriches every garden plot either individually or in groups, even when situated in half-shade or soil lacking nutrients. The light flowers contrast nicely with dark backgrounds. It is recommended for borders of woody beds.

SIMILAR VARIETIES: Many other "Spring Roses" originated under the care of the German cultivator Kordes. All of

them have strong fragrances and grow up to 6 ft (2 m) tall. These are "Frühlingsanfang" (simple, white flowers, many hips), "Frühlingsmorgen"(simple, cherry-red with yellow centers, many hips) and "Frühlingszauber" (lightly packed, light-red with yellow centers).

STEWED HIPS
Soak 10½ tbsp of dried hips in 2 cups of water for several hours. Then pour half the water off and add 1 cup of white wine and around 1 cup of sugar. Cook for 5 minutes, stirring constantly. The stewed hips can be enjoyed in desserts or pancakes.

"Händel" Rose

Location:

☼

Qualities:

❀❀ ♪

ORIGIN: Cultivation, McGredy 1965.

APPEARANCE: Upright, richly branched shrub; grows 5 ft (1.5 m) tall and wide, climbing even taller in mild climates.

FLOWERS: The loosely packed flowers are silver-white and have wide, pinkish-red rims. Their petals are wavy and give the rose a romantic charm. The individual flowers are about 3 in (8 cm) wide and spread a light fragrance. They appear continuously all summer. They contrast nicely with the dark-green, nearly purple leaves.

SPECIAL QUALITIES: This sporty variety, with stunning, two-colored flowers, is always a curiosity among Shrub Roses. One of its parents is the red-blooming climber "Gruß an Heidelberg," from which it inherited its striking appearance.

USAGE: An eye-catcher in any garden, either individually or in small groups. This variety can be also grown as a climber. It looks especially good on columns and pyramids.

"Jacqueline de Pré" Rose

ORIGIN: Cultivation, Harkness 1989.

APPEARANCE: Upright, bushy, quickly growing, 4 ft (1.2 m) tall, up to 5 ft (1.5 m) wide.

FLOWERS: The big, lightly packed flowers are ivory-white and have eye-catching, reddish golden anthers. They have diameters of about 4 in (10 cm) and resemble clematis in shape. Their intense, musky fragrance is unique. Many flowers appear above the dark-green leaves, and the plant blooms luxuriantly after the main blooming period.

SPECIAL QUALITIES: A sporty rose that also enjoys nutrient-deficient soil.

USAGE: Owners of small gardens will enjoy this compact shrub, which is also nice as a potted plant. It is suitable for low hedges due to its substantial width.

SIMILAR VARIETIES: The simple, white flowers of "Rosenzauber" (32 – 40 in/ 80 – 100 cm) have a pink touch.

Location:
☼

Qualities:
✿✿ ჳ

Usage:
🪴

"Lavender Lassie" Rose

Location:
☼ – ☼

Qualities:
❀❀ ✿

Usage:
🗑 ✂ ✗

ORIGIN: Cultivation, Kordes 1960.

APPEARANCE: Upright, bushy, 5 ft (1.5 m) tall, about 4 ft (1.2 m) wide.

FLOWERS: The large, full flowers are lavender-pink and contrast nicely with the dark-green leaves. The wavy petals lend an antique charm to the dense, cup-shaped, fragrant flowers. The flower clusters appear continuously until fall.

SPECIAL QUALITIES: The rose is low-maintenance and pretty. It tolerates half-shade and soil lacking in nutrients and humus. Its leaves are healthy and not very susceptible to fungal diseases.

USAGE: "Lavender Lassie" is ideal for small gardens because of its compact appearance. It is suitable for loose hedges, enjoys pots and can be used as a climber too.

SIMILAR VARIETIES: The strong, full, fragrant flowers of "Rosenresli" show a color play of orange-pink to crimson-red. This variety can border lanes as well.

"Lichtkönigin Lucia" Rose

ORIGIN: Cultivation, Kordes 1966.

APPEARANCE: Upright, bushy branched, 3 – 5 ft (1 – 1.5 m) tall, up to 35 in (90 cm) wide.

FLOWERS: The bright lemon-yellow, full flowers appear from early summer to late fall. The lightly fragrant individual flowers have a diameter of 3 – 4 in (8 – 10 cm) and grow in many umbels. They contrast beautifully with the glossy, green leaves. The yellow buds with reddish stripes are just as attractive as the flowers.

SPECIAL QUALITIES: This robust and very frost-resistant variety is one of the few shiny yellow Shrub Roses. It was awarded an ADR predicate in 1968.

USAGE: This attractively shaped Shrub Rose, nice individually as well as in groups, is recommended for loose hedges. It tolerates sunny, hot locations as well as half shade and harsh climates. It brightens up the dark borders of woods. It is suitable as a potted plant and its flowers last a long time in a vase.

Location:
☼ – ☼

Qualities:
✿✿ ♪

Usage:
🪣 ✂

"Maigold" Rose

Location:

☀ – ☀

Qualities:

Usage:

ORIGIN: Cultivation, Kordes 1953. A hybrid of *rosa spinosissima* (see *pimpinellifolia* above).

APPEARANCE: Upright, bushy shrub, well branched especially at the top, quickly growing, long hanging shoots, many thorns, 6½ – 8 ft (2 – 2.5 m) tall and wide.

FLOWERS: The loosely packed flowers are golden-yellow with a touch of copper. They look like loose, flat clusters when open. They are quite big, with diameters of 3 – 4 in (8 – 10 cm) and they give off a strong fragrance as well. They appear from May to June, either individually or in clusters. Several light blooms follow after a luxurious main blooming period in early summer.

SPECIAL QUALITIES: It is recommended to prune the plant in a timely manner (preferably after blooming) so as not to lose leaves from bellow.

USAGE: This bushy Shrub Rose, which tolerates half-shade, needs much space for its overhanging branches to be clearly visible. It is ideal to keep the distance between plants at 6 ft (3 m). It is more suitable as a solitaire, but you can also grow it as a climber.

"Mein schöner Garten" Rose

ORIGIN: cultivation, Kordes 1997.

APPEARANCE: upright, bushy, branchy, 3 – 5 ft (1 – 1.5 m) tall.

FLOWERS: The salmon-pink, loosely packed flowers with light centers get lighter towards the rims. They grow in umbels and appear continuously all summer. They are accompanied by a fruity fragrance. The dark-green, glossy leaves contrast nicely with the sporty flower color.

Location:
☼ – ☼

Qualities:
🌸🌸 ⌎

Usage:
▦

SPECIAL QUALITIES: This praised variety combines ample flowers and a romantic, yet healthy and robust flower shape. "Mein Schöner Garten" grows in hot, sunny locations as well as in half-shade and the flowers keep their shape even in rain.

USAGE: It is also an eye-catcher individually, but the floral beauty is more intense in groups. Because it does not grow so big, the rose is suitable as a potted plant or for larger graves.

SIMILAR VARIETIES: The pink-blooming "Dornröschenschloß Sababurg" spreads a romantic charm and a Wild-Rose-like fragrance.

"Parkjuwel" Rose

ORIGIN: Cultivation, Kordes 1956.

APPEARANCE: Upright, bushy, many branches, quickly growing, 6 – 6 _ ft (1.5 – 2 m) tall and 6 _ – 8 ft (2 – 2.5 m) wide.

FLOWERS: The big, densely packed, fushia flowers develop from beautiful, mossy buds. They are round, about 5 in (12 cm) across and appear in June and July. They emit a pleasant fragrance. The old-fashioned flowers look especially bright above the dark leaves.

SPECIAL QUALITIES: Its parent is an unknown red Moss Rose from whom the variety inherited its flower shape, mossy buds and stalks. Moreover, it is not high-maintenance and grows in soil lacking in nutrients and in half-shade.

USAGE: If you have much room, you can plant this "wide" park rose as an eye-catching solitaire. It is also suitable as a climber and for tall hedges.

SIMILAR VARIETIES: "Parkzauber" is a bit smaller and blooms shiny fuchsia-red.

"Park Wilhelmshöhe" Rose

ORIGIN: Cultivation, Kordes 1987. A hybrid of *rosa gallica.*

APPEARANCE: Wide shrub, quickly growing, overhanging branches, 32 – 40 in (80 – 100) cm tall.

FLOWERS: The cup-shaped, dense, full flowers are bright, crimson. It revives the charm of Old Roses with its loose, bushy shape.

SPECIAL QUALITIES: A robust park rose with many romantic Old Rose blossoms.

USAGE: It grows wide and its beauty is best displayed when the variety is planted individually.

SIMILAR VARIETIES: "Sir Henry," an offspring of *rosa rugosa*, features dense, full, purple-lilac flowers with antique charm. Its flowers have a strong fragrance and the bushy plant grows to 3 ft (1 m) tall.

Location:
☼

Qualities:
❀ ♪

Usage:
✄ ✗

"Pink Grootendorst" Rose

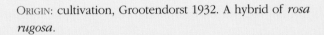

Location:

Qualities:

Usage:

ORIGIN: cultivation, Grootendorst 1932. A hybrid of *rosa rugosa*.

APPEARANCE: stiff, upright, dense and well-branched in its upper part, shoots with many thorns, 3 – 5 ft (1 – 1.5 m) tall and wide.

FLOWERS: The full flowers are pink in efflorescence and turn light-pink later. Their diameters are only about 1 ½ in (4 cm), but they grow in big clusters above glossy green leaves. This variety blooms from June to August and once again, less lusciously, in the fall.

SPECIAL QUALITIES: This old variety has lost none of its charm.

USAGE: You can plant this multi-functional rose individually, in small groups or in hedges. The distance between the plants (3 – 6 ft/1 – 2 m) determines the size. It reaches 28 – 32 in (70 – 80 cm) in hedges. It also tolerates half-shade.

SIMILAR VARIETIES: "F.J. Grootendorst" is a red counterpart.

"Polka 91" Rose

ORIGIN: Cultivation, Meilland 1991.

APPEARANCE: Upright, bushy, well branched, 4 ft – 5 ft (1.2 – 1.5 m) tall.

FLOWERS: The dense, amber-yellow flowers have an old-fashioned shape. 2 – 3 flowers grow on a stem, reaching about 3 in (7 cm) in diameter and have an intense fragrance.

Location:

Usage:

ROSE SALAD

Try to combine various salad varieties with rose petals. You can also add flowers of daisies, dandelions, bitter cress or whatever else you find in your garden. Make a vinegar-oil dressing and sweeten it with honey or apple juice.

SPECIAL QUALITIES: This modern Shrub Rose has a romantic character. It will charm you with its unusual color, symmetric appearance and lovely fragrance. It is a "Romantic Rose" by the French cultivator Meilland.

USAGE: It is striking alone or in a group. Plant 2 plants, at most, per square yard/meter.

"Pure Caprice" Rose

ORIGIN: Cultivation, Delbard 1997.

APPEARANCE: Bushy, quick growing, 32 – 40 in (80 – 100 cm) tall.

FLOWERS: The half-full flowers show an interesting color change from yellow to pink and finally to green. The petals are fringed on the rim and give the flower an untidy look. The anthers are visible in the middle. The flowers contrast nicely with dark-green, thick leaves.

SPECIAL QUALITIES: One of the frost-resistant, noble Wild Rose cultivars with a tender fragrance by the French rose expert Delbard.

USAGE: This compact variety is suitable as a Shrub or Bed Rose. It is a good choice for small gardens and for pots. It is always an eye-catcher, either individually or in groups.

SIMILAR VARIETIES: The flowers of "Citron-Fraise" (3 – 5 ft/ 1 – 1.2 m) are all different. Some of them are just pink, others nearly white or bi-colored. They are always half-full and emit a tender fragrance. Lovers of strong fragrances will adore "Malerrosen" by the same cultivator. They are

introduced as "Paul Cézanne" under Noble Roses.
"Fragrant Provence Roses," by Meilland, has a French
charm.

ROSE LIQUEUR

**Petals of fragrant roses are best suited for drinks with a rose
aroma. Put 20 petals of fragrant roses, 3 cups of white rum
and 1 cup of white sugar into a sealable pot. Then put the pot
in a cool place for 6 weeks and stir the contents regularly.
Filter the liqueur once more and pour it in a decorative bottle.**

"Romanze" Rose

ORIGIN: Cultivation, Tantau 1984.

APPEARANCE: Upright, wide shrub, 3 – 5 ft (1 – 1.5 m) tall and about 32 in (80 cm) wide.

FLOWERS: The shiny pink, full flowers with wavy petals bloom from drop-shaped, red buds. They are quite big, with diameters of 4 – 5 in (10 – 12 cm). This variety blooms until late fall. It emits a subtly sweet fragrance.

SPECIAL QUALITIES: A robust, frost-resistant rose, which tolerates full sun as well as half-shade. Its flowers withstand showers without serious problems. It was awarded an ADR predicate in 1986.

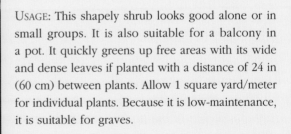

USAGE: This shapely shrub looks good alone or in small groups. It is also suitable for a balcony in a pot. It quickly greens up free areas with its wide and dense leaves if planted with a distance of 24 in (60 cm) between plants. Allow 1 square yard/meter for individual plants. Because it is low-maintenance, it is suitable for graves.

"Scharlachglut" Rose

ORIGIN: Cultivation, Kordes 1952. A hybrid of *rosa galli-ca.* Syn. "Scarlet Fire."

Location:

Qualities:

APPEARANCE: Upright, wide shrub, overhanging branches, quickly growing, 6 ft (2 m) tall and wide, sometimes even taller.

FLOWERS: The simple, cup-shaped, shiny scarlet-red flowers have yellow-gold anthers in the middle. They reach diameters of 4 – 5 in (8 – 10 cm) and are grown individually in most cases. Their blooming period is June through July and they have a tender fragrance.

FRUIT: Many round hips of a glossy cherry-red in the fall.

SPECIAL QUALITIES: A rose shrub with an eye-catching color and impressive dimensions which needs a lot of space. It tolerates half-shade and soil lacking in nutrients.

USAGE: This wide-growing variety also needs much space as an individual (plant at a distance 10 ft or 3 m apart). You can plant it in big gardens and parks or in small groups. It also likes to climb small trees.

"Schneewittchen" Rose

Location:

☼ – ☀

Qualities:

🌼🌼 ☽ 🌿

Usage:

🪣 🌱

ORIGIN: Cultivation, Kordes 1958. Syn."Iceberg," "Fée des Neiges."

APPEARANCE: Upright, wide shrub with overhanging branches, 3 – 5ft (1 – 1.5 m) tall.

FLOWERS: Shiny, white, full flowers with diameters of 3 in (8 cm). They have a light fragrance and form big, loose umbels. The blooming period begins early in summer and continues until fall.

FRUIT: Many hips.

SPECIAL QUALITIES: A classic among white Shrub Roses – frost-resistant, rain-resistant and resistant to most diseases. It tolerates full sun as well as half-shade and attracts many bees and other insects. It was praised in 1960.

USAGE: This low-maintenance variety can be successfully combined with roses of other colors and perennials thanks to the neutral color of its flowers. You can plant it individually as well as in groups and it offers a blooming frame in a hedge. It looks good as a potted plant and especially good as a tree.

SIMILAR VARIETIES: The full flowers of "Vogelpark Walsrode" do not shine pure white, but charm you with a tender porcelain-pink so delicate that it is nearly white. It is as multi-functional as "Schneewittchen." "White Gold" is a new, white variety with big, full flowers, "White Nights" blooms a creamy white.

ROSE HIP TEA

This is an effective remedy for colds. It cleans the blood, has a diuretic effect and boosts the metabolism. First, dry the hips in an oven at 212°F/100°C until they burst. It is best to put them on baking paper first. Soak 1 teaspoon of hips in 1 quart of water for 10 minutes and then filter.

"Weiße Wolke" Rose

Location:

Qualities:

Usage:

ORIGIN: Cultivation, Kordes 1993.

APPEARANCE: Wide shrub, bushy, 35 in (90 cm) tall, 28 in (70 cm) wide.

FLOWERS: The pure white flowers are dense, full and cup-shaped. The shiny yellow anthers will catch your eye. The individual flowers are very big with the diameter of 4 in (10 cm). The big clusters cover the dark-green, glossy leaves almost completely. They have a lovely, sweet fragrance.

SPECIAL QUALITIES: A cloud of flowers and fragrance for large areas or small gardens.

USAGE: This rose is impressive alone. It quickly makes large areas green with its wide and dense leaves. It is suitable for low hedges and big pots too.

SIMILAR VARIETIES: "Pearl Drift" is an English variety of 1980, an offspring of the "New Dawn" climber. Its white flowers are soft pink and the plant is a bit bushier than "Weiße Wolke." Both Shrub Roses are alike in other qualities as well.

"Westerland" Rose

ORIGIN: Cultivation, Kordes 1969.

APPEARANCE: Upright, wide bush, well branched, compact; 5 – 6½ ft (1.5 – 2 m) tall.

FLOWERS: The shiny, apricot-colored flowers turn a light pink when wilting. They are half-full and open like cups. They reach a diameter of 4 in (10 cm). The luxurious umbels have a strong fragrance.

SPECIAL QUALITIES: Hardly any other variety has the unusual hue of this rose. It is low-maintenance, tolerating hot, sunny locations and the flowers are not damaged badly by rain. It was praised with an ADR predicate in 1974.

USAGE: A spot of color in any garden, individually, in groups or in hedges. You can use it as a potted plant too.

SIMILAR VARIETIES: "Belvedere" charms you with huge, dense, orange-apricot flowers. The half-full flowers of "Bonanza" are golden-yellow with coppery red rims.

Location:
☼

Qualities:
❀❀ ⌣

Usage:
🪣 ✂ ✕

PURELY NATURAL WITH WILD ROSES

Wild Roses are once-blooming shrubs with simple flowers, bred from seed or plants. They grow 3 – 10 ft (1 – 3 m) tall and are often classified as once-blooming Shrub or Park Roses. The pure varieties are better suited for bigger gardens and the countryside, thanks to their luxurious growth, while others also grow a bit smaller. They can be striking individually, will protect hedges against wind and reinforce hillsides. Wild Roses bring a bit of pure nature and wilderness to your garden. They enrich the animal world with lots of pollen and many hips. You can also make delicious food and drinks from the vitamin-packed fruit. If you have Gallica Rose or *rosa rubiginosa* in your garden, you can pick the big hips. Unpruned plants grow to be big and dense, with many thorns, offering shelter for birds and other small animals. The shiny, red thorns of *rosa omeiensis pteracanta* are very festive. Wild Rose lovers prefer the ecological benefits of a rose to an eye-catching flower color and shape. The hybrid varieties of *rosa rugosa* are very popular with hoverflies, which are natural enemies of aphids. Surprise yourself by the variety of Wild Roses.

Rosa Gallica

ORIGIN: Gallica Roses are in Central and southern Europe as far as West Asia at home.

APPEARANCE: Bushy, but compact shrub. It spreads, thanks to underground rootstalks. Up to 3 ft (1 m) tall and 20 in (50 cm) wide.

FLOWERS: Dark pink to light red with shiny, yellow anthers. The flowers are simple and cup-shaped and their diameter is about 3 in (7 cm). They grow individually or in groups of two or three. They bloom once between June and July and spread a light Wild-Rose-like fragrance. You can see the "Versicolor" Gallica Rose in the picture.

FRUIT: Reddish brown, ball or pear-shaped hips with glandulous hair.

SPECIAL QUALITIES: This wild variety is one of the oldest garden roses ever and is the "mother" of many cultivated varieties. It is low-maintenance and well-suited for nearly all natural gardens where it is a natural shelter for birds.

Versicolor *Gallica rose*

USAGE: This bushy Wild Rose is suitable for big areas individually or in groups. It is ideal for hillsides because it stabilizes them. Moreover, it is a very robust plant and perfect for lining roads. It loves sunny places and chalky soil, but does not tolerate shade from trees or sandy soil well. Plant 1 – 2 flowers per square yard/meter.

VARIETIES: The pale pink, half-full flowers of "Versicolor" ("Rosa Mundi") have lively, crimson-red stripes. "Belle Isis" charms you with its pink flowers, myrrh-like fragrance and is ideal for smaller gardens. "Hippolyte" has purple-violet flowers and grows 5 ft (1.5 m) tall and wide. "Violacea" catches your eye with its velvety, dark-red, loosely packed and lightly fragrant flowers. It is also known as "La Belle Sultane."

Rosa Moyesii
Mandarin Rose

ORIGIN: Bloody Rose – as the variety is also called thanks to the shiny color of its flowers – comes from western China and was introduced in Europe in 1894.

APPEARANCE: Upright, a very wide shrub, 6½ – 10 ft (2 – 3 m) tall and up to 6½ ft (2 m) wide. It has only a few thick main shoots which branch at the tops.

FLOWERS: The simple, purple-red flowers are cup-shaped and 1 – 2 in (3 – 5 cm) in diameter. They grow along the shoots, individually or in groups of two or three. Blooms once in June.

SPECIAL QUALITIES: This shrub has many shiny, orange-red, bottle-shaped hips. The fruit is very big, about 2 in (4 – 5 cm) long. This frost-resistant shrub offers food for birds with its many hips. It is also a beloved bee-pasture and tolerates half-shade.

USAGE: This shrub is impressive alone, but you can plant it in groups too, if you have enough room.

It is recommended for natural gardens. Plant 2 plants per square yard/meter at most. Because it also grows in acid soil, it can be well integrated into heather gardens.

Varieties: Some interesting varieties have arisen thanks to breeding. One of them is "Nevada," with creamy white, loosely packed flowers. You can enjoy a second bloom in the fall after the main blooming period in June and July. "Highdowensis" blooms with simple, dark-pink flowers. "Marguerite Hilling" is full of clusters of loosely packed, pink flowers and is not hanging.

Rosa Multiflora
Multiflora Rose

ORIGIN: This wild variety from Japan and Korea was introduced in France in 1860, where it played a role in the cultivation of amply blooming Bed Roses, such as Rosa Polyantha.

APPEARANCE: Bushy shrub, many branches, quickly growing, 6 _ ft (2 m) tall on average, sometimes even taller. Its shoots are elegantly hanging and bent.

FLOWERS: The small, white flowers develop from equally small, white buds. They are around 1 in (2 – 3 cm) wide and consist of five petals. They grow in big, pyramid-like blooms, eye-catching above glossy, green leaves. The blooming period is June and July. They spread a light, honey-like fragrance.

FRUIT: there are many ball-shaped hips, but they are just less than ½ an inch in diameter.

SPECIAL QUALITIES: This Multiflora Rose earns its name since its big flower clusters consist of up to 50 blossoms.

Usage: Ideal for tall hedges and for stabilizing hillsides when planted in groups. A distance of 3 – 5 ft (1 – 1.5 m) between plants is recommended. It can also stand individually in a garden and it looks best in natural gardens. Rosa Multiflora is a well-used, robust base for cultivation.

Cultivation of Roses

In bud grafting, the bud (eye) of a noble variety is grafted onto the root collar with a T-shaped cut. This is best done in summer. Bind the grafting spot with bast fibers and prune the wild variety the following spring.

Rosa Rubiginosa
Sweet Briar

Location:

Qualities:

Usage:

ORIGIN: The Wild Rose, native to Europe and West Asia, has been cultivated since the middle of the 16th century. It is also known as "Apfelrose," "Schottische Zaunrose" or "Sweet Briar."

APPEARANCE: An upright shrub with overhanging shoots with many thorns, quickly growing, 6½ – 10 ft (2 – 3 m) tall, up to 6½ ft (2 m) wide.

FLOWERS: The simple, pink, cup-shaped flowers, with light centers and diameters of 1 – 2 in (3 – 5 cm), usually grow in groups of two or three on the tops of shoots and spread a light fragrance. They bloom once in June – July.

FRUIT: Many scarlet-red hips of less than 1 inch (1 – 2 cm) remain on the plant until winter.

SPECIAL QUALITIES: This rose offers food and shelter to birds. It is popular with insects because it sheds lots of pollen. If you crush the dark-green, matte, feathery leaves, they emit an apple-like fragrance.

USAGE: A Wild Rose grown individually or in groups for natural hedges. It is a good choice for natural gardens and for planting in the country. You can combine it without problems with other Wild Roses or Woody Plants. Keep distance among individual plants of 28 – 40 in (70 – 100 cm) in hedges and allow even more space for individuals (5 – 8 ft/1.5 – 2.5 m). It can also be striking in pots.

HIP HARVEST IN FALL

Harvest them from September to October when the fruit is already bright red but not yet hard. Cut them, removing the insides and drying in the air. Seal them tightly in jars and you will have a rich stock of vitamins for the winter

Rosa Serica

Rosa Omeiensis Pteracant

ORIGIN: Rosa Serica, Silk Rose, from China, was introduced in Europe in 1890. *Rosa omeiensis pteracanta* is an offspring of a wild variety. From the botanical point of view, it is a variety of a cultivar (*rosa serica subsp. omeiensis fo. pteracantha*).

APPEARANCE: This quick growing shrub has many branches and grows 6½ – 10 ft (2 – 3 m) tall and wide. It spreads through its rootstalks.

FLOWERS: The simple, white flowers are relatively small, with a diameter of ½ – 1 ½ in (2 – 4 cm). But they appear

in plenty above the glossy green, feathery leaves. They are special because they very often have four instead of five petals. They sprout many shoots and are usually planted individually. The blooming period starts in summer.

FRUIT: Many small, red hips.

SPECIAL QUALITIES: This rose is an eye-catcher from a distance thanks to the red, shiny thorns that gave this rose its name. They usually appear on young shoots and are less than 1 in (1 – 2 cm) across.

USAGE: This highly frost-resistant Wild Rose looks best when planted individually. Hedges of *rosa omeiensis pteracanta* quickly develop into thick barriers and are beloved as shelters by birds. Because the plants grow very luxuriantly, you need lots of space in your garden for them.

PRICKLES OR THORNS?
Roses have prickles, outgrowths of the plant's skin-like epidermis. A prickle can be easily broken off. Thorns are modified parts of the plant, such as leaves or branches.

Rosa Spinosissima
Burnet Rose

ORIGIN: The Wild Rose, native to Europe, is often seen on northern coasts and is also known as "Dünenrose." It was recorded by botanists earlier than *Rosa Pimpinellifolia.*

APPEARANCE: Bushy shrub, upright with slightly hanging shoots with many thorns, 3 – 5 ft (1 – 1.5 m) tall and wide. The shrub spreads through rootstalks.

FLOWERS: The simple, cup-shaped flowers are a tender cream color and have a sweet, honey-like fragrance. They appear plentifully from May to June.

FRUIT: The violet-black hips are a unique aspect of this rose.

SPECIAL QUALITIES: It tolerates sand and salty, nutrient-deficient soil and is often used to stabilize hillsides.

USAGE: Individually, it is certainly stunning in your garden. It creates lovely natural hedges when planted in rows. 1 – 2 plants per square yard/meter are enough for a loose floral carpet.

The Burnet Rose is a beloved bee-food and also grows well in half-shade. It is suitable for hillsides and heather gardens too.

Varieties: "Frühlingsgold" blooms golden-yellow and emits a sweet fragrance. "Frühlingszauber" has light red flowers with attractive yellow centers and an intense fragrance. "Maigold" is characterized by golden-yellow, full flowers with a coppery touch and a strong fragrance. These varieties are, at 8 – 10 ft (2.5 – 3 m), a taller variety and they can also grow as climbers on climbing structures. "Stanwell Perpetual" charms you with its loose, full, pinkish flowers and beautiful fragrance.

SMALL SPACES FOR MINIATURES

When you think of roses, do you think of luscious country gardens, romantic rose-arches and hidden arcades? Luckily, we don't need to live in a movie or on an enormous estate to enjoy the beauty of roses because Miniatures are small enough for even the smallest places. At the same time, they make up for their short height of no more than 12 – 20 in (30 – 50 cm) with bounteous flowers. Miniatures look good in pots, planters and containers. Make sure that the container is at least 10 in (25 cm) deep and wide so that the plants have sufficient room to grow. They need water and nutrients regularly. Plant Miniatures in beds and on patios and they are suitable for rocky gardens and graves as well. You should not combine them with quick growing perennials or woody plants, however, because they will lose their dramatic visual effect. Patio Roses, as Miniatures are sometimes called, are less robust than Bed Roses and need more attention. Their small, tender leaves are more susceptible to fungal diseases, especially black spots arising from soil. The smaller the plant, the greater its susceptibility to disease. Prevention is the best medicine here as well: place the plants in a sunny, airy location and never water them on their leaves. Cultivated Miniatures are recommended for gardens because they are much more robust and more grow better than pot roses.

"Mandarin" Rose

ORIGIN: Cultivation, Kordes 1987.

APPEARANCE: Bushy, compact, about 10 in (25 cm) tall.

FLOWERS: The loosely packed, lightly fragrant flowers are orange-yellow in the center and turn salmon-pink towards the rim. They are very big, with diameters of 3 – 4 in (8 – 10 cm), in comparison with their short shoots and small leaves. They contrast nicely with the glossy, green, thin leaves.

SPECIAL QUALITIES: An eye-catcher with two-tone flowers, which appear in umbels and give the rose a romantic charm.

USAGE: "Mandarin Rose" is suitable for balcony pots and other planters. You can also plant them in border and flower beds, but be sure there is only one variety in a bed or just other Miniatures. Otherwise, the small plants will quickly be overgrown.

SIMILAR VARIETIES: "Bunter Kobold" (12 – 16 in/ 30 – 40 cm) blooms yellow and red with many colors. The orange, full flowers of "Pan" have asymmetric, yellow stripes.

"Orange Meillandina" Rose

ORIGIN: Cultivation, Meilland 1980.

APPEARANCE: Upright, bushy, densely branched, 12 – 16 in (30 – 40 cm) tall.

FLOWERS: The shiny, orange-red, full flowers develop from drop-shaped, salmon-pink buds. They open cup-shaped and have diameters of about 2 in (4 cm). The red flower clusters contrast strongly with the thin, glossy green leaves. This variety blooms repeatedly during a long blooming period.

SPECIAL QUALITIES: The shiny flowers keep their hue a long time and have many color accents. Tree miniatures are very decorative as well.

USAGE: These miniatures are suitable for planting in groups in beds, on patios, along paths and in flower pots of all types. Under optimal conditions, they do not require much care. The distance between plants should be 12 in (30 cm) about 8 – 10 plants per square yard/meter.

SIMILAR VARIETIES: "Cumba Meillandina" blooms orange, "Peach Meillandina" apricot-orange, and "Sunny Meillandina" yellow.

Location:
☼

Qualities:
❀❀

Usage:
🪴 🌱

"Rosmarin 89" Rose

ORIGIN: Cultivation, Kordes 1989.

APPEARANCE: Bushy, strongly branched, but compact, only about 8 in (20 cm) tall.

FLOWERS: The pink flowers are densely packed and rain-resistant. The umbels appear all summer with one significant main blooming period. They grow above dark-green, very dense leaves. The drop-shaped buds are red and the flowers are pink.

SPECIAL QUALITIES: "Rosmarin" is one of the smallest Miniatures. The rosette-shaped, full flowers give it a romantic charm.

USAGE: A beautiful Miniature for balcony pots, planters and containers. It is also available as a tree miniature. You can plant it individually or in groups in a garden, but it needs an optimal location. An ideal distance between plants is 12 in (30 cm); 8 – 10 plants per square yard/meter are recommended. Low, quickly growing perennials complement it. This variety is also suitable for planting on graves.

Similar varieties: "Charmant" (12 – 16 in/30 – 40 cm) charms you with pure pink, rosette-shaped flowers and a sweet fragrance. The pinkish red, dense, full flowers of "Amulett" (20 – 24 in/50 – 60 cm) resemble pompon dahlias. "Dresden Doll" (12 – 16 in/30 – 40 cm) is a miniature Moss Rose. The mussel-pink, full flowers open from many mossy buds.

Ancestors of the Modern Miniatures

Origin: Thanks to their small size they adapted excellently to the countryside and the climate in China. They came to England in 1810 and were initially popular as a house plant. The present garden varieties have been cultivated and thus are more robust than their ancestors.

"Sneprinsesse" Rose

Location:

Qualities:
❀❀ ⌇

Usage:
🗑

ORIGIN: Cultivation, Grootendorst 1966.

APPEARANCE: Bushy, upright, about 14 in (35 cm) tall.

Flowers: The full, white flowers are round in shape. They are relatively small and have a tender fragrance. They compensate for their small size with many dense clusters growing above light-green, glossy leaves. This variety blooms repeatedly.

SPECIAL QUALITIES: "Schneeprinzessin" is characterized by very healthy leaves. This attractive Miniature is an offspring of the well-known Bed Rose "Muttertag."

USAGE: A low rose for flower and border beds, balconies and pots. The white flowers catch the eye when planted in groups. It is recommended to keep a distance between plants of 14 in (35 cm).

SIMILAR VARIETIES: "Schneeküsschen" also charms you with small, white flowers touched with pink. They grow 12 in (30 cm) tall. "White Gern" is nice with its dense, full, white flowers. The red "Muttertag" complements the colors nicely, just like "Orange Muttertag."

"Sweet Dream" Rose

ORIGIN: Cultivation, Fryer 1988. Syn. "Frymincot."

APPEARANCE: Bushy, upright, about 18 in (45 cm) tall.

FLOWERS: The dense, full flowers are a bright apricot-peach color. They open cup-shaped and spread a delicate fragrance. The leaves are dense and glossy and contrast beautifully with the warm color of the flowers.

SPECIAL QUALITIES: This is a variety of Patio Rose that fills the space between Miniatures and Floribunda Roses excellently. They are bigger, bushier and more robust than Miniatures and will charm you with their dense, rosette-shaped flowers.

USAGE: Ideal for flower and border beds in small gardens, planting on patios or balconies and in pots. Big roses, behind or among a group of low Patio-Roses, catch the eye.

SIMILAR VARIETIES: "Apricot Clementine" also grows compactly, with full, pink-apricot flowers.

Location:
☼

Qualities:
✿✿ ↶

Usage:
🪣

"Zwergenfee" Rose

Location:

Qualities:

Usage:

ORIGIN: Cultivation, Kordes 1979.

APPEARANCE: Bushy, loosely branched, medium-quick growing, about 14 in (35 cm) tall.

FLOWERS: The shiny red, velvety-glossy flowers are dense, full and rosette-shaped. They grow in clusters of 3 – 5 blossoms on thin shoots and have a pleasant fragrance. The individual flowers are very big, with diameters of 2 in (5 cm). The buds are a deep blood-red, unlike the flowers.

SPECIAL QUALITIES: The cheerfully-colored flowers look good from a distance. The leaves are reddish in efflorescence, matte green later. They contrast strongly with the red petals.

USAGE: This small rose is suitable for pots of all types. It is best planted in groups so that the floral beauty is clearly visible in flower and border beds. Suitable for rocky gardens and graves. It is generally recommended to keep the distance between individual plants at 12 –14 in (30 – 35 cm), i.e., 9 – 11 plants per square yard/meter.

Similar varieties. "Maidy" grows 12 in (30 cm) tall and wide. It has big, full flowers of scarlet-red with eye-catching, silver-white lower surfaces. It is recommended for balcony pots and 4 plants have enough room in a 3 ft (1 m) planter. The scarlet-red flowers are half-full and appear copiously in dense umbels until late fall.

FANCY MIXES WITH SUMMER PLANTS AND PERENNIALS

Roses are beautiful alone, but if you like vivid colors, plant summer flowers and perennials among your Miniatures. Slowly growing plants are best here, e.g., sweet alyssum, bellflower or herbaceous perennials from rocky gardens.

"Zwergkönig 78" Rose

Location:
☼

Qualities:
✿✿

Usage:
🪴 ⚘

ORIGIN: Cultivation, Kordes 1978.

APPEARANCE: Bushy, upright, well branched, 16 in (40 cm) or taller.

FLOWERS: The shiny, crimson-red flowers are well-packed and open cup-shaped. They have a diameter of 2 in (5 cm). The intense color contrasts with the dark-green leaves. This repeatedly blooming variety has a very long main blooming period.

SPECIAL QUALITIES: This robust Miniature is suitable for small gardens as an alternative to Bed Roses.

USAGE: An important Miniature for pots and balconies, available as half-trees and miniature trees as well. You can plant it individually or in groups in your garden, in flower and border beds. It is suitable for low hedges as well as for graves, but remember to keep a distance between plants of 12 – 14 in (30 – 35 cm).

SIMILAR VARIETIES: "Alberich" is equally multi-functional, but has small, deep crimson flowers which bloom in a pyramid shape.

"Zwergkönigin 82" Rose

ORIGIN: Cultivation, Kordes 1982.

APPEARANCE: Wide shrub, upright, 14 –16 in (35 – 40 cm) tall.

FLOWERS: The intense pink flowers bloom from round, crimson-red buds. They are rosette-shaped, full and open cup-shaped. They are very big in comparison with other Miniatures with diameters of 2 – 2½ in (5 – 6 cm). They contrast nicely with the very glossy leaves, even though they lose color when wilting.

SPECIAL QUALITIES: This pink-blooming sister of "Zwergkönigin 78" is similarly multi-functional and robust. It has a romantic charm with its wavy petals and tender fragrance. It shows big, floral clusters during the main blooming period, with flowers appearing very often individually during the second bloom as well.

USAGE: A Miniature equally suitable for flower and border beds and for potting. It looks stunningly beautiful in your garden when planted in bigger groups. It is also available as a half or miniature tree.

Location:
☼

Qualities:
❀❀❀ ↻

Usage:
🪣 ↕

Register

Aachener Dom 104
Abraham Darby 126
Adélaide
  d' Orléans 192
Akkerroos
  (bosroos) 220
Albaroos 40, 46, 50,
  58, 152
Alchymist 194
Amber Queen 68
American Pillar 195
Angela 224
Anne Harkness 69
Apothekersroos 8, 52,
  255-256
Aprikola 70
Aspirin-Rose 162

Ballade 71
Ballerina 164
Barkarole 105
Baron Girod
  de l'Ain 30
Belle Epoque 106
Belle Story 128
Bernstein Rose 72
Bischofsstadt
  Paderborn 225
Blanche Moreau 32
Blaze Superior 196
Bonica 82 74
Bordure Nacrée 75
Bosroos (akker-
  roos) 220

Bourbonroos 44, 62
Bright Smile 76

Centifolia 38, 50,
  56, 59
Charles Austin 130
Charles de Mills 34
Charles Rennie
  Mackintosh 132
Chinaroos 54, 65
Colette 226
Compassion 197
Comte
  de Chambord 36
Constance Spry 134

Damascenerroos 42
Dark Lady 154
Darthuizer Orange
  Fire 227
Dirigent 228
Dornröschen 229
Dortmund 198
Duftzauber 84 107
Duinroos 234, 266

Easy Going 77
Edelweiß 78
Egelantierroos
  255, 262
English Garden 136
Erfurt 230
Erna
  Grootendorst 79

Erotica 108
Escapade 80

Fair Play 165
Fantin-Latour 38
Felicitas 231
Ferdy 232
Flammentanz 200
Fleurette 166
Flirt 81
Focus 109
Franse roos 255, 256
Freisinger
  Morgenröte 233
Friesia 82
Frühlingsduft 234

Gallicaroos 34, 52, 64,
  134, 256
Gärtnerfreude 167
Gelbe Dagmar
  Hastrup 168
Gerbe Rose 202
Gertrude Jekyll 137
Gloire de Dijon 203
Gloria Dei 110
Golden
  Celebration 138
Goldener Olymp 204
Goldmarie 82 84
Graham Thomas 139
Great
  Maiden's Blush 40
Gruß an Aachen 85

Händel 236
Harlekin 206
Heckenfeuer 86
Heckenzauber 87
Heidekönigin 170
Heidetraum 171
Heritage 140

Ispahan 42

Jacobietenroos 46
Jacqueline de Pré 237
Jayne Austin 142
Japanse bottelroos
  (rimpelroos)
  169, 176

Kir Royal 207

La Sevillana 88
Lavender Dream 172
Lavender Lassie 238
Leander 143
Leonardo da Vinci 90
Leverkusen 208
Lichtkönigin Lucia 239
Lilli Marleen 91
Louise Odier 44
Lovely Fairy 173
Lykkefund 209

Magic Meidiland 174
Maigold 240
Mandarin 270

Manou Meilland 92
Mary Rose 144
Max Graf 176
Maxima 46
Mein schöner
  Garten 241
Mme Hardy 48
Mme Legras de St.
  Germain 49
Montezuma 112
Mosroos 32-33, 50, 51,
  242, 272
Morning Jewel 210
Mozart 178
Muscosa 50
Muttertag 94

NDR 1 Radio
  Niedersachsen
  Rose 95
New Dawn 211
Nostalgie 96
Nuits de Young 51

Officinalis 8, 52, 61
Old Blush China 54
Orange
  Meillandina 271
Othello 146

Painted Moon 113
Palmengarten
  Frankfurt 179
Park
  Wilhelmshöhe 243
Parkjuwel 242
Paul Cézanne 114
Paul Noël 212

Pink
  Grootendorst 244
Polarstern 115
Polka 91 245
Pompon
  de Bourgogne 56
Portlandroos 36, 60,
  61, 137
Pretty Jessica 148
Pur Caprice 246

Queen Mother 97
Queen of Denmark 58

Raubritter 213
Redouté 150
Remontantroos 30-31
Rimpelroos (Japanse
  bottelroos) 169, 176
Robert le Diable 59
Romanze 248
Rosa canina 40,
  46, 75
Rosa chinensis 8,
  54, 65
Rosa gallica 34, 52,
  64, 256
Rosa indica 54, 65
Rosa moschata 178
Rosa moyesii 258
Rosa multiflora
  67, 260
Rosa pimpinellifo-
  lia 266
Rosa rubiginosa 262
Rosa rugosa 168-169,
  176, 243, 244, 255
Rosa sericea 264

Rosa sericea
  Pteracantha 264
Rosa spinosissima 266
Rosa x alba 40, 46,
  49, 58
Rosa x borboniana
  44, 62
Rosa x centifolia 38,
  50, 56, 59
Rosa x centifolia mus-
  cosa 32, 51
Rosa x damascena
  36, 42, 48, 60, 61
Rosa x damascena
  var. semperflo-
  rens 30
Rosarium
  Uetersen 214
Rose de Rescht 60
Rose du Roi 61
Rosemary
  Harkness 116
Rosenprofessor
  Sieber 98
Roseromantic 180
Rosmarin 89 272
Rote Flamme 216
Rote Max Graf 181

Samba 99
Savoy Hotel 117
Scepter d'Isle 151
Scharlachglut 249
Schneewittchen 250
Schwarze
  Madonna 118
Sea Foam 182
Sebastian Kneipp 119

Shropshire Lass 152
Silver Jubilee 120
Sneprinsesse 274
Sommerabend 183
Sommermorgen 100
Sommerwind 184
Souvenir de la
  Malmaison 62
Suma 186
Super Dorothy 217
Swany 187
Sweet Dream 275

The Dark Lady 154
The Fairy 188
The Pilgrim 156
The Prince 157
Trier 2000 101
Tuscany 64
Typhoon 122

Valencia 123
Veelbloemige
  roos 260
Veilchenblau 218
Venusta Pendula 220
Viridiflora 65

Weiße Wolke 252
Westerland 253
Wife of Bath 158
Winchester
  Cathedral 159

Zwergenfee 276
Zwergkönig 278
Zwergkönigin 279